Healing The Sexually Abused Heart

A Workbook For Survivors, Thrivers, and Supporters

By Dr. Jaime J. Romo

CREDITS

Publisher:	Dr. Jaime J. Romo
Publishing & Design Consultation:	Kirk Whisler
Cover Design and Artwork:	Maja Dale
Editorial & Design Assistance:	Melanie Slone

ISBN 978-188937938-8

WPR PUBLISHING
2777 Jefferson St., Ste. 200
Carlsbad, CA 92008
760-434-1223 fax:760-434-7476
kirk@whisler.com

DEDICATION

"Social religion is perfected when private religion is purified. The body becomes stronger as its members become healthier. The whole church of God gains when the members that compose it begin to seek a better and higher life."

— A.W Tozer, *The Pursuit of God*

I have been blessed to know and experience the support of many survivors, most of whom cannot be named here. Nonetheless, I wish to thank Barbara Blaine and David Clohessy for their courageous work in bringing this horrible chapter in our history to light, so that clergy sexual abuse everywhere can be seen and understood and ended. I thank Mary Grant, who was the first survivor to reach out to me and let me know that I was not alone. Thanks to Jeannie Wills, who shared her critical and hopeful perspective in the developmental writing stages of this book.

I also wish to thank Dr. Richard Sipe, who has been a mentor, friend and ally for me ever since we met at a press conference. Margaret Schettler has been a kind and thoughtful colleague in creating spaces for this material to be used and improved. Both have been examples of prophetic presence, sometimes comforting the afflicted and sometimes afflicting the comfortable.

This workbook is dedicated to everyone who wishes to end child sexual abuse. In particular, it is dedicated to my wife and children, who have walked with me through my darkest hours and have inspired me to live.

TABLE OF CONTENTS

MY SPIRITUAL METAMORPHOSIS

INTRODUCTION

I recently heard a presentation about quantum shifts in consciousness, as well as in technology, that are appearing around the world. The speaker discussed nanotechnology and environmental breakthroughs, such as edible clothing in New Zealand and window panes in Scotland that extract energy from the wind and sun. He was particularly excited about recent scientific discussions about the metamorphosis of a butterfly.

While I don't recall the technical details, I do remember that I was impressed with how similar the story he told was to my own spiritual life journey. I'll approximate the story, conscious that it is not a perfect scientific explanation, but with the understanding that it describes a spiritual process that may be useful for others as they struggle with the impact of abuse by religious authorities at individual or a collective level. In short, it is inaccurate to say that a butterfly is a caterpillar with wings. Similarly, it is inaccurate for me to describe myself as a religious or spiritual person with simply more wisdom than I had before dealing with the religious authority sexual abuse in my life.

The caterpillar develops as a caterpillar does. It crawls and eats and produces other caterpillars. However, at one point, it eats a tremendous amount, and then spins a cocoon around itself. During the time the caterpillar is in its cocoon, a radical decomposition takes place. Cells begin to consume and digest one another and to bring about chemical changes to the caterpillar, in effect, destroying the caterpillar as it once was. During this process, some cells in the caterpillar body remain dormant and do not interact or react with this decomposition or chemical reaction. These are now being called "imaginal cells".

When the decomposition process has run its course, the various imaginal cells reawaken and begin to work together to reconstruct what will become a butterfly. I don't know how this happens, but it was intuitively obvious to me. The speaker gave the analogy of taking a bicycle that needs repair to a bicycle repair shop and coming back a few days later. But instead of a new bicycle, the repair shop worker presents a jet and says, "Here you are." While they may have some common elements and material similarities, in reality there is a quantum leap in this new construction from what it once was.

MY PROFESSIONAL JOURNEY

From the time I left seminary in 1984, I worked towards the dream of bringing social justice and the incarnation of God into the world through education. I am familiar with other educators' stories, such as Dr. Henry Trueba, an educational giant in many scholars' eyes, who also brought their spiritual journeys to education.

"Influenced by Paulo Freire and my colleagues associated with him (Donaldo Macedo, Moacir Gadotti, Peter McLaren, Henry Giroux, and many others) I began to deconstruct my previous experiences. I soon realized that I was still a priest, and that my commitment to students' intellectual growth was advocated in lieu of my previous vocation to proselytize and convert, and in lieu of nurturing spiritually Christian souls, I would nurture the intellectual life of students." (Romo, Bradfield, and Serrano, 2004, p. 28.)

I was also a zealous and dedicated advocate for kids, working under the vision of bringing institutional transformation that would promote equity and inclusion and the realization of social justice in practice and policy. I worked for 23 years as a middle and high school teacher, as a middle and high school administrator, and as a university teacher education professor. Similarly, my religious zeal manifested itself in my life in an informal Christian community, where we shared resources and ministry to refugee and homeless families. When I married, I worked in retreats and was active in my local parish and youth ministry. My wife and I took our children to work in the parish soup kitchen regularly. When we became less satisfied with the traditional liturgies and dogmatic practices, we participated in a home church group led by a married priest.

As a professor, I invested more time and effort to research-innovative teaching practices and scholarship, and I had less involvement with parish activities. During the summer of 2002, I participated in a week-long program called The Collegium. It was a gathering of faculty who worked at Catholic Universities. We discussed various topics related to academic life in the context of Catholic universities. During this time, the clergy abuse scandal from Boston was in the news daily.

My flashbacks began around that time. Some memories of my abuse were triggered by seeing my sons sleeping shirtless; they were about the age I was when I was abused. I had some basic and crude understanding of my abuse at that point, which I mistakenly interpreted as life experiences that I could manage or had processed indirectly in previous therapy related to family-of-origin issues such as alcoholism or the relationship with my father.

Later that summer, I called a phone number on the L.A. Archdiocesan Web page to let someone know what I thought he or she must want to know in order to help others. I got a message that the call could not be completed. I searched the Web page for an e-mail contact or other phone number to call someone about my report. I e-mailed the Web master, the only contact I could find, and the Web master reported back to

me that he had forwarded the information to the appropriate person. On my birthday, I received a call from the diocesan Victims' Assistance Coordinator, who asked me what I wanted.

This was during what I consider the prime of my academic career. I was published, teaching well, and involved in statewide and international teacher education conferences and research. During the course of the next year, I contacted an attorney who advised me to file a police report and who put me in touch with the local leader of the Survivors Network of those Abused by Priests (SNAP). That spring, I drove between San Diego and Los Angeles Counties to attend support meetings, where I heard my own story in graphic detail through many others' stories.

The following summer, again on my birthday, I met with other survivors who were organizing outreach and advocacy efforts in southern California. They told me what they wanted to do and asked me to help. With great trepidation, I led a leafleting campaign outside the San Diego Police Department and led my first press conference shortly afterwards. I began leading efforts to draw attention to abuse at local parishes, regular press conferences, and support meetings. I also wrote letters to newspaper editors and began fielding regular calls by victims of clergy abuse. All of this activity fell under my vision of bringing social justice and to protect children; it was service to my community.

In part, it was a way to channel the rage that was consciously opening up in me. My depression and rage made it difficult to manage my emotional land mines. I was working at Catholic University, where the bishop sat on the Board of Trustees. I was aware that some trustees questioned the supportability of any faculty member who might be involved with clergy abuse in the diocese. I was driven to earn tenure, to establish a new educational research field called Border Pedagogy (i.e., examining complex educational and sociopolitical issues involved in the San Diego-Tijuana region), and to bring accountability within all churches, beginning with the Catholic Church, related to clergy abuse.

During the fall of 2005 I was diagnosed with Post Traumatic Stress Disorder (PTSD). I dragged myself to a psychiatrist for this diagnosis when I could no longer conceal or deny to myself that I could not read or effectively remember lectures and educational material that had become second nature to me over the previous ten years of teacher education. I was on emotional edge in my Catholic university environment, working and conflicting with tenured colleagues who reminded me of church hierarchy. During the spring of 2006, I took a medical leave of absence and worked intensively with therapy and medication to get better.

I returned to my work at the end of the spring of 2006, and resumed my research, conference management, and teaching full time in the fall. Shortly after the 2006-2007 academic year ended, I received notification that I would not be reappointed, which circumvented my bid for tenure. I had just co-directed an international conference. The notice was a kind of dagger into my heart. I appealed to the Provost and my appeal was denied. I was encouraged by activists in the clergy abuse community to sue the University. I believe the suit would have been "won", if that can be assessed. But I did not sue. I had worked for four years with the frustration of the legal process with the Catholic Church and I refrained from pursuing more legal action, contrary to my fresh desire for revenge.

MY SPIRITUAL METAMORPHOSIS

When I recently heard the story about the metamorphosis of the caterpillar to the butterfly, I recognized my own metamorphosis. I had overindulged in public advocacy, media contact, mentoring and trying to get more activism out of survivors than they were able or willing to give with respect to their own abuse. In other words, I was burned out from calling people to come to press conferences or to speak up, so that more faces than my own would be identified and heard with respect to ending abuse.

During my activity as an advocate and spokesperson for clergy abuse victims, I became involved with a local United Church of Christ (UCC) church. I was desperate and spiritually starved. I missed the bliss I once had known

from my seminary days and I was alienated from what was once my spiritual and social justice community. At a more basic level, I lost whatever I had known as peace of mind.

My leave of absence in 2006, before I had begun meditation, became my cocoon from my life of being a victim and a survivor, which was both validating and clarifying, as well as limiting. This life as a victim or survivor was validating because it was the first time I could see how my abuse could happen, how it had impacted me, and how I had impacted others. It was limiting because I could not relate to others in a more expansive way, and it was emotionally toxic. My leave was a valuable, intensive time to convalesce, and reconcile and integrate my various experiences, roles, and ways in which I identified myself. In retrospect, this process set the stage for me to move forward in a very different way.

During this time, my new church became known nationally when a registered sex offender came to it and asked to be permitted to worship there. I took up a role of a spiritual support team member, and met with this person weekly. That experience was re- traumatizing, as well as being one of the more significant efforts that I had ever made towards reconciling painfully different perspectives and letting go of my own sexual abuse trauma cocoon.

In February of 2008, my wife and I participated in a Chopra Center program called "Healing the Heart." I went out of pure frustration and desperation with my professional and marital life. The program impacted me profoundly and I felt some of the rage lift from my spirit. The program introduced me to Primordial Sound Meditation, and I began a regular meditation practice that gave me some simple peace of mind. Two months later, I participated in a six-day program that was meditation intensive.

I would describe this as my spiritual metamorphosis process, wherein the tensions of being a survivor and a survivor advocate, as well as my various emotional demands, deconstructed who I was. By the time I participated in the six-day meditation program, I was as good as dead. Or at least my identity as a teacher educator and tenure-track faculty member and Border Pedagogy researcher was dead. It was then that the imaginal cells, my spirit — God's Spirit — began to bring about a new state of being in me. Since then, I have continued in this expansive process. At this point, my meditation practice is a way for me to breathe and expand spiritually, like a butterfly opening and closing its wings while resting.

CLOSING THOUGHTS

Meditation has helped me learn some very important spiritual lessons in the past several months: That my life is unfolding and made up of pure potentiality, if I'm flexible, willing to change, learn, and apply what I learn; that I need to take care of myself before I work effectively with others; that it is more important for me to be happy, with my mind, heart and soul connected, than disconnected and right— the first takes more time.

I've learned that peace is possible and difficult, as it requires lots of letting go and re-writing the scripts that have been so familiar for so long. I have learned that I am much more than my titles, positions, possessions, or experiences —good and bad. Therapy and emotionally healing processes have helped to sift out and let go of ways of thinking or behaving that are not useful to becoming something else, something bigger. I believe that this letting go process is critical for the expansive process that comes through my spiritual practice to be transforming at quantum levels.

The quantum shift shows me that I am. Before life and after death, I am. I think I understand what Marianne Williamson wrote:

> *"You are a child of God.*
> *Your playing small doesn't serve the world.*
> *There's nothing enlightened about shrinking so that other people won't feel insecure around you.*
> *We are all meant to shine, as children do.*
> *We are born to make manifest the glory of God that is within us.*
> *It's not just in some of us, it's in everyone.*
> *And as we let our own light shine, we unconsciously give other people permission to do the same.*
> *As we are liberated from our own fear, our presence automatically liberates others."*

My point in sharing some of my life experience is that, because I have developed a deeper clarity about who I am, I have been able to move forward with a deeper happiness and peace than I ever imagined possible at the beginning of my abuse flashbacks. Just as it is inaccurate to say that a butterfly is a caterpillar with wings, it is inaccurate for me to describe myself as a religious or spiritual person with simply more wisdom than I had before dealing with the religious authority sexual abuse in my life. I am honored to walk with you in your journey of healing.

Peace,

Dr. Jaime J. Romo

Share your thoughts on this book & possibly win prizes.
Everyone who shares ideas on how to make this workbook better will get a free copy of the next edition of the book.
Go to www.HTSAH.com or www.HealingTheSexuallyAbusedHeart.com

HOW TO USE THIS WORKBOOK

Two expressions come to mind related to this workbook. The first is, "the map is not the territory". This workbook (i.e., spiritual map) is a synthesis of various bodies of knowledge that range from learning theory, to spiritual development, to leadership development, to applied psychology, to healing and recovery. In that way you may find some familiar methods in "journaling" or self assessment. However, I bring these various methods to a territory that has been unmapped, for the most part. That territory is the virtual or internal universe (spiritual life) as impacted by religious authority sexual abuse. As is the case with any map, this workbook is only partially useful in identifying landmarks, but does not have or adapt to the details that you, the reader, will necessarily bring from your own life experiences in particular contexts.

This recalls the second saying introduced by one of the greatest educational leaders of the past century, Paulo Freire: "To read is to coauthor the text." Freire proposed the revolutionary goal of literacy for all people, which would empower people to read not only the word, but also the world (i.e., the meanings, messages and systems behind the written word), so that readers would become change agents of their own lives. Any lesser form of literacy, for him and me, leads to a kind of oppression or imprisonment.

This workbook is a guide, ideally used in conjunction with other forms of guidance, whether they are mental health professionals, trusted and competent spiritual guides, or established communities of learning and recovery from religious authority sexual abuse. In that way you will make the connections for yourself that will make the material more relevant and useful for you in your particular journey.

I recognize that there are many different spiritual paths that have brought many people to include this workbook in their journey towards healing. Nonetheless, I suggest some guidelines for using this workbook:

1. **Start at the beginning.** This may seem obvious or silly, but I say this as someone who has too often rushed to the conclusion or finish line without spending the important time to understand the foundational concepts and processes, or internalize them as a result of participating in a learning process. If nothing else, reading the first chapters will make subsequent learning clear, if not more productive.

2. **Work within your limits.** Just as it is possible to get hurt by over-asserting physically, it is possible to become overwhelmed or strained emotionally by taking on too much too soon. I suggest that you work in the workbook every day for a small amount of time. If you cannot work every day, work every other day. The reconstructive process and critical thinking development process require time to integrate and transform past limited or misinformation into new, applied learning that can be useful here and now.

3. **Be skeptical, but not judgmental.** Often lost in the popular anti-intellectual culture of lazy skepticism is a healthy skepticism. Bring your questions and experiences to the material. Ask how it might be useful or true, especially when it does not immediately seem useful with respect to your experience. However, do not rush to judgment or conclusion, as you are embarking upon a deep learning process which often feels like

disorientation, confusion, or even incompetence. By allowing yourself to accept your learning process as part of your healing process, you will find answers to the question of how the material might be useful or true for you.

4. **Give yourself the same patience, encouragement, and respect** as you would give to another person who is doing something difficult the first time, whether it be a child learning to ride a bike or to read, a runner training for a marathon, or a colleague finishing a degree in advanced studies. You are embarking on a profoundly significant healing and transformation process. A mentor congratulated me when I was completing my doctorate: "It's not what you've done, but who you have become." You will become more whole and alive than you may have thought possible, given the life experiences that bring you here today.

For those recovering from religious authority sexual abuse in any way, we may feel spiritually parched, like the ground in a drought. Little to nothing will grow in us that leads to joy or enthusiasm, both spiritual experiences that were once available to us, at our core. This book is a tool to help you to reconnect to that core and to quench your spiritual thirst, and then to go on to have those blessings poured like water over you. This book recognizes that the spirit's need to be blessed is as urgent as the body's need for water.

Part 1 of this workbook is written with and primarily for victims or survivors of religious authority sexual abuse. Overall, the direction of the first four chapters might be: mourning the past, mourning the present, choosing to live, and living. The chapters are organized to facilitate the readers' thinking process by examining: the experiences related to the recovery process (what), the action logic that supports the respective experiences (how), the implications of working through this stage of the process (so what?) and finally, next steps related to this stage (now what?). This format is theoretically grounded in my background as a teacher educator and action researcher. Each chapter addresses a different state of spiritual recovery or healing, and some of the ways we can notice how our hearts and minds may be out of alignment with one another (e.g., voices in our head, responses to authority, boundaries, roles, and critical thinking levels).

If you need a time line to begin with, give yourself 90 days to read and work with the first four chapters, maybe even a month per chapter. This isn't a race, although the urgency to regain the enjoyment and enthusiasm that comes from our soul may tempt us to go faster or to expect more of ourselves than is good for us. As I've been advised about meditation time, don't rush into these spiritual exercises and don't rush coming out of them. Let go of the hopes that doing something faster is better, or the beliefs that becoming familiar with information is the same as learning. Thank you for taking this step in your spiritual revival and liberation, and for being, as Gandhi once said, "the change you wish to see in the world."

Part 2 of this workbook is written with and primarily for survivor supporters, whether or not they have experienced sexual abuse by a religious authority. Chapter 5 is informed by sociological discussions about racism and the ways that people knowingly and unknowingly participate in it. While the terms (systems theory) and categories (cheerleader, bystander, and ally) are borrowed from another field, they are no less useful in understanding the complexity of this taboo topic. I believe that the first four chapters may also be useful for survivor supporters, in order to better understand stages of recovery for survivors. At the end of the workbook, I have included some definitions of words I have used in each chapter.

The map is not the terrain. This workbook offers an imperfect map related to uncharted territory: healing hearts from religious authority child sexual abuse. I offer it humbly and with gratitude that others will bring their experience and knowledge to this territory. I offer it with hope that it will spark dialogues among survivors and survivor supporters, and that it will help others to find their way.

Caminante, no hay camino. El camino se hace al caminar.
Traveler, there is no road. We make the road as we walk.

Dr. Jaime J. Romo

CHAPTER ONE
VICTIMS

INTRODUCTION

I went to a homeless shelter recently to deliver some clothes and furniture to any families who might need them. I don't know if the few people I made eye contact with were representative of everyone in this group, but I imagined that I saw deep despair or shame in those faces. It reminded me of five years earlier, the first time that I walked into a meeting with other adults who had been abused by religious authorities, in the spring of 2003. At that moment, I felt a strange kinship with the people I saw, who seemed, in my mind, tormented. The good and bad news in this workbook is that you are not alone.

A couple of years after my first encounter with other victims of religious authority sexual abuse (RASA), I recalled that meeting in an article I wrote for a local "Call to Action" newsletter in 2005. Here is an excerpt from it:

> I heard recently that another victim committed suicide after he learned that his criminal case was being thrown out of court because he reported the molest after the statute of limitations allowed. His mother said that when the case was thrown out of court, her son lost hope. He lost a sense of being heard, understood, believed, and that any real change would come about as a result of his abuse. I understand his need to see a change come as a result of my and hundreds of people's experiences. I understand what it's like to feel insane, holding a secret that no one wants to hear, and feel as though, if I can't be believed about something at the core of my life experience, that I practically don't exist.

Going to support meetings has been like going to a cancer ward and seeing that I'm a member. That's where I've seen the looks of silenced frustration, buried rage, and profound betrayal and understood myself in a way that I hadn't seen before. That's where I volunteered to stand in front of police stations, churches and the convention center to hand out leaflets to encourage others to come forward and report abuse, to take up their role, their responsibility in this reform. It terrifies me to be public about this issue when I work in a Catholic university. A recent revelation that we have hate crimes at the university shocked many. It didn't surprise me because I know that abuse happens in environments where the language and explicit values are lofty (social justice, service, community) and the established authorities are conservative, patriarchal and unaccountable.

THINK: VICTIM, HEAL THYSELF

This chapter is for victims of religious authority (i.e., guru, imam, minister, monk, nun, priest, rabbi, etc.) sexual abuse (RASA) who want to recover, heal and live. Since we're talking about healing, we're talking about a change in our self understanding, which is a beginning step towards becoming healthy. You can change tires on the car and change clothes. You can change toothpaste, or you can change your mind about something. When we talk about physical, mental, and spiritual health, we're really dealing with transformation. Changing appearance or expressions is very temporary and superficial. Flexibility of heart or mind leads to transformation, a shift in **who we are** that impacts **how we live**. Transforming the body, a way of thinking, or spiritual life is the deeper work of the Spirit in us.

If it had an origin, this workbook would be a response to a challenge, "Victim, heal thyself." This workbook is for you to use, as it is helpful to understanding the profound questions that have confounded so many of us who have been sexually abused by religious authorities (i.e., religious men and women, and others who represent God). The profound questions I refer to are: Who am I? What do I want? What is my best self's contribution to the universe?

For those of us who have been sexually abused by a religious authority, these questions may be distinctly difficult as we may be in different stages of mourning everything we have understood about our spiritual selves in our particular religious settings. This process can lead to a more sophisticated understanding of who we are, if we are willing to think more critically about ourselves and the religious cultures in which we were sexually abused. Victims of RASA mourn the loss of knowing what we know or thought we knew about

spirituality, as shaped and reinforced by religious authorities, oftentimes our families, communities and perhaps even educational or governmental institutions. This mourning process can move us to acknowledge and later reconcile the profound splitting in our bodies, minds, hearts, and souls, related to RASA.

I hope that the voice I have found in my recovery, combined with the perspective I bring from my professional development, will help you find your own voice and expand your own perspective about your worth and role in helping to protect children and vulnerable adults. Let's begin with an exercise that relates to waking what might seem to be a sleeping or unconscious spirit in us as victims. The exercise might seem unusual or be difficult, as it addresses a foundational question that victims may not have even wanted to answer, given the deep spiritual pain that victims have absorbed and carried for so long. After the exercise, I'll give some background about why it is so important and perhaps so difficult for adults who were sexually abused as children by a religious authority, male or female, Buddhist, Catholic, Hindu, Jewish, Muslim, Protestant, sect or other.

ACT 1.01: WHO AM I?

This exercise is about you in the here and now. It doesn't relate directly to religious authority sexual abuse (RASA) per se. Later in the chapter, we'll address RASA in the context of there and then. The idea in this exercise is for you to fill in as many different ways as you can while naturally answering the same question, and not to come up with a "right" answer. Victims, because of our coping skills, too often look at things in the either-or, right or wrong mode. Part of the purpose of this exercise is to practice being more flexible in how we see ourselves.

After coming up with your list of responses, you will be able to assess them with a sponsor, therapist or another person whom you trust. Even if you don't have someone in mind at this point, do the exercise, as it will spark a shift in your thinking about yourself and your well-being now.

Who am I?

Who am I?

Who am I?

Who am I?

Who am I?

Who am I?

Who am I?

Who am I?

ACT 1.02: FLEXIBILITY

For each of our answers to the question, "who am I?" we carry many descriptors or scripts in our mind about what that means, what we should do or should expect as _____. For the purpose of offering an example, I can share that, for me, as a father, I have worked with a deep, often unconscious belief that I should have all the answers for my children or that I should be strict and overprotective, since the parenting I got was the opposite.

Choose any of the answers you gave. Answer the following questions with your "who are you" identity in mind. The exercise is intended to help you begin to have a new and improved (i.e., transformed) version of that self. Answer the following:

How can I be more flexible when dealing with unfamiliar or uncomfortable ideas?

When is it okay for me to be more flexible with unfamiliar or uncomfortable ideas?

What might be some benefits to my being more flexible with unfamiliar or uncomfortable ideas?

What might I lose as a result of not being flexible with unfamiliar or uncomfortable ideas?

What negative things might happen or continue to happen if I am not more flexible?

What is keeping me from becoming more flexible?

What am I willing to do in order to be more flexible?

What do I commit to now in order to be more flexible?

ACT 1.03: HAPPINESS

Are you happy? To whatever degree you can answer, "yes", you can point to a seed of happiness that can grow, flower, and be fruitful if it is nurtured. Yes, I'm speaking from the experience of religious authority sexual abuse, physical and spiritual rape. In reality, each of us can participate and find the benefits of transformation every day and in many ways. Choose the same answer that you used in the first exercise and answer the following questions.

Am I happy with my current state or experience as _____?

To what degree am I willing to ask for or to accept help from others who can assist me in becoming the person I want to be?

Which image that I have created or accepted of myself am I willing to let go of?

Where did I get that image I have of myself?

If there are some aspects of this self-image and self-understanding that are life-giving, am I willing to let go of the rest?

What is keeping me from letting go of a self-image that brings me unhappiness as _____ (or getting help in doing so)?

What might I gain by transforming my experience as _____?

What might I lose if I don't transform my experience as _____?

REFLECT: RECOVERY

Congratulations on the work you have done that has led you to this point in your recovery. I hope this workbook has engaged you in your own experience, as our experience is valuable, albeit most painful, in this early, "victimhood" stage of recovery. You are not alone. I and many others understand what it's like to feel insane, holding a secret that no one wants to hear: That your abuse happened in a religious environment, where the language and explicit values were lofty and the established authorities represented God, and were unaccountable.

The exercises you have worked with are difficult for anyone; it makes sense that they are even more difficult for someone whose "here and now" is full of pain. The exercises deal with intellectual and spiritual development, and each of us is at a different level of this development. In the following pages, I'll present information that will give you a context or map that will add to your own understanding of: What happened; how abuse happens in religious environments; what some distinctive impacts of abuse by religious authorities are; and what you can do to promote your own healing and spiritual life.

SECTION ONE
WHAT HAPPENED?

Regardless of the details, and the details are important, what happened is that we were physically or sexually abused, or both, by a religious authority. Someone who we believed to represent God used his or her physical, social, or cultural authority, crossed boundaries, and used us as an object. That abuse may have been violent and painful. That abuse may have been through seduction. Some victims of sexual abuse by a religious authority remember the abuse in clearly defined terms (i.e., for a particular period of time, number of times, etc.). Some don't. We may have been unconscious or under the influence of drugs or alcohol. Don't call it a relationship. It didn't start "innocently", whatever "it" was. At some point, we were victimized.

Before religious authority sexual abuse took place, there was probably a grooming process or some kind of mind control that allowed this person or persons to use us as objects. Many victims recall a prolonged "grooming" process, which seems more personalized, wherein victims develop an extraordinary trust in the abuser, even an extraordinary familiarity with and care for the abuser. This grooming period may have taken months or years before the sexual abuse, in whatever manner, was enacted. This grooming process renders some victims

defenseless, as they conclude that the abuse is or was normal. Others live with a conflict that God is involved or approves of the abuse, which effectively renders the abuse indefensible.

I don't know any victim of religious authority sexual abuse who doesn't share the dilemma that the abuser was "all mighty": beyond reproach, beyond limits, beyond being brought to some human accountability. In short, the abuser was God-like, all mighty. Not almighty, of course, but all mighty. Religious authority abusers were people whom parents, grandparents, or respected community leaders admired. The abuser was called by God and formally ordained to be God's representative on earth. The abuser may have been part of an institution that could elevate him or other religious authority to the highest seat in this world-wide organization: the papacy. The abuser was all mighty. This is quite a bind to be in, wherein a victim cannot really fight this authority of authorities, nor can a victim physically escape from the abuse. It makes sense that one response is for a victim to close off from his or her soul or experience his or her deepest self as dead. This would make it extremely difficult to answer the question in the opening exercise, "Who am I?"

THINK: A CHILD'S WAY OF COPING

Some children and vulnerable adults might try to make sense of their experience the following way, without even knowing that this process is going on:

1. I am being hurt by an adult in authority or a trusted adult.
2. This must be the result of one of two things: Either I am bad, or the adult or person in authority is bad.
3. As a child, I have been taught to obey adults, that adults in authority are always right and are doing things for my own good.
4. Therefore, it must be my fault that I am

being hurt. I must deserve this.
5. Therefore, I am bad, as any other explanation says my parent is bad and this is unacceptable. I have been hurt because I am bad.
6. I am hurt often so I must be very bad.

In addition to whatever charisma or charm the abuser exercised with us, he or she was a person who we and our families and church members believed had the authority to interpret God's word. The abuser was a person who carried the church's religious story forward. In other words, the abuser was the keeper of the "word" that was the connecting thread among all members of this shared religious identity. In a sense, the abuser was all knowing. Therefore, when an abuser of this status, stature, and authority sexually violates a child or vulnerable adult, it is incomprehensible by the abused.

But most devastating is the decapitation from our own spirit or soul that comes with religious authority sexual abuse. What happened to me and so many others who were sexually abused by a religious authority was that before, during, and after the abuse, we were silenced, and then we silenced ourselves so that we would not feel the devastating impact to our conscious living, or to our psyche, our deepest and unconscious self. In effect, we adopted a "no talk" rule in our lives. A traumatized child or vulnerable adult reacts in such a way as a coping skill to try not to be hurt even more in a religious setting in which we read, understand, and do what we're told in order to be right with God, our religious leaders, and religious community members. This is not the healthy behavior of a person in a healthy environment that protects children or vulnerable adults from religious authority sexual abuse.

ACT 1.10: UNDERSTANDING WHAT HAPPENED

This activity requires you to recall your abuse, to whatever degree you can. The activity may push your buttons or get you worked up, emotionally speaking. It is intended to help you gain more insight about yourself and what happened to you, and thus allow you to more effectively respond (you choose an appropriate behavioral response) rather than react (your emotions dictate your behavioral response) to that person's inappropriate behavior. Follow the format outlined below to help you with this process.

1.   Situational Context (Who, what, when, where, why)
In a brief paragraph, describe or outline the circumstances involving you, the person, and any other players.

2.   Triggers (external and internal); the trigger can be both external and internal.
The internal trigger refers to your emotional state prior to the situational context. For example, if you left home in an uptight mood because of a fight with a parent or sibling, your thoughts and emotions may have been focused on this experience; therefore, you may have been in an emotional state when you walked into the context in question.
External triggers refer to the other person's behaviors that led to the abuse. What did he or she say that led to the abuse? What behaviors did he or she engage in?

3.   Physiological Response
Under stress, the body produces cortisol and adrenaline, chemicals that can contribute to a fight-flight-freeze response. As the brain stem controls reflexive responses, your body may have responded with an accelerated heart beat, higher blood pressure, tense muscles, changed breathing pattern, sweating, etc. What was your bodily response to the abuse?

4.   Self-Talk

What did you say to yourself every time when this person engaged in behavior that led to the abuse or during the abuse? It's okay, in this assignment, to confess that you actually entertained a few choice swear words to describe how you were feeling at that particular point in time. It's very important that you bring to consciousness the self-talk you typically engage in, more so under the stress produced with religious authority sexual abuse.

5.   Emotions

Which feelings come to the fore? Anger? Anger is usually a secondary response, as underlying anger is a mixture of other feelings that are already being contaminated by your internal trigger or mood prior to this encounter. Underlying anger are such feelings as annoyance, irritation, hurt, grief, etc.

6.   Behavioral Response

What was your first behavioral response to this person's behavior? Did you ignore him or her because you weren't too sure how to handle him or her? Did you order him or her to leave your presence?

7.   The effect of your behavior on the other

How did your response affect the other person? How did he or she, in turn, respond to you? How did your response change over a period of time?

REFLECT: WHAT HAPPENED TO YOU?

What insight about yourself did this person pass on to you? How did you change?

I continued to participate in church life as an adolescent and young man. I embraced the gospel of respect for life, solidarity with the poor and social justice. I found an intellectual connection with "liberation theology", even as I was disconnected from my own spiritual death. After graduating from college, during which time I maintained a reckless and accidental spiritual life (participating in music ministry while numbing myself from deeper emotional or spiritual life), I had a "conversion experience". I attended a Catholic seminary for three years, in search of a fully committed spiritual life in the church in which I lived, moved, and had my being. After I left the seminary, I was involved in a lay retreat movement, called Cursillo. My wife and I were married in the old Los Angeles Cathedral, surrounded by hundreds of Cursillistas and friends who saw us as the next generation of lay leaders. All of this made sense as long as I was not conscious of my sexual abuse by my parish priest.

My individual story is one of thirty in Carmine Galasso's book, *Crosses: Portraits of Clergy Abuse*. What happened then for many in this distinctive collection is that we left our bodies, or disassociated from the experiences. We experienced a spiritual death, which led to self-loathing, depression, paranoia, drug or alcohol abuse, violent behavior, and self-destructive or near death experiences. Many developed a belief in being worthless, or of worthlessness, and became suicidal. Many viewed themselves as a prostitute. Many developed health or diet problems, hair or skin problems, or self-mutilation behaviors. Many lived with profound shame, damaged relationships, and damaged employment, or a combination of these factors. Many acted with oppositional behavior, and some experienced imprisonment as a result of their behavior.

ACT 1.11: Healthy Behavior

Healthy behavior is more responsive than reactive. Take some time to think about how this description fits with your experience, now that you are an adult. Consider how your experiences of abuse relate to the answers you gave in response to the question, "Who are you?" Write, draw, paint, or express in whatever creative way you can how those past experiences impacted your identity or sense of self. This may be an out of workbook activity.

THINK: FINDING OURSELVES IN AN EMERGENCY ROOM

In the following example, I use physical health as a way to think about recovery and healing that also relates to our own mental, emotional, and spiritual health. I am speaking in very general terms, and I recognize that there are many particular circumstances around each person's mental, emotional, and spiritual health. I encourage you to take what is useful from the following analogy and to let go of what is not useful.

Imagine that a person finds herself in an emergency room for a health-related matter (e.g., because she has been in an accident, or for some health breakdown that has been building over time). There is certainly a need for immediate intervention (e.g., someone else may need to operate on the patient), as the patient is unconscious. After that initial intervention, the patient may need to take certain medications or, in the case of diet-related issues, begin using pre-designed food packages or a nutrition or health program to get her body functions stabilized. Given this stage of recovery (especially if the person has practiced poor decision-making that led to the health crisis), it is understandable that a patient follows someone else's health orders. The patient is temporarily dependent on another person in order to be told what to do and how to do it to get healthy. This is what I think the expression, "Give a person a fish and she eats for a day; teach a person to fish and she eats for a lifetime" relates to. Transformation, and health in this general analogy, relates to learning to manage our own bodies, minds, and spirits.

ACT 1.12: WHO AM I? PLEASE ANSWER THE FOLLOWING:

Who am I and who do I want to become?	
Now:	Future:
What is the same?	
What is different?	

THINK: WHEN THINGS FALL APART

The metaphor helps me understand my own experience of seeing my life fall apart, despite my hard work or good work I did before the memories crashed into my present. I didn't want to be depressed or angry; I just was. I didn't want to lose the skills I had developed to solve problems and be productive in society; I just did. I didn't want to accept that my life had become unmanageable, even more unmanageable than I had thought I had addressed through therapy or 12-step programs; I just had to. I was the patient. I had no idea how many others were helping me or of the degree to which others were supporting me. I didn't know and I didn't want to know. I was furious about what had happened and what was happening. There's nothing flattering about being a victim. I know no survivors of religious authority sexual abuse who want to be seen as a victim of RASA. But by recognizing that we are where we are, we can begin to regain, and eventually manage, our health.

After an accident's initial treatment and convalescence, our recovery and health is in our hands. Perhaps it means that we do not engage in high-risk or any risky behaviors. Perhaps it means that we learn about different foods and pay attention to our own bodies, so that we can exercise and eat in ways that make sense for us.

Perhaps it means that we learn about different healthy relationships and learn to manage our emotional, interpersonal, or professional boundaries. Perhaps it means that we consider our mental and spiritual health as critical aspects of our well being. We can always learn from others' programs, expertise, experience, and stories. That, in fact, is what this workbook is about. As victims, our critical thinking skills are low: We have been conditioned to "not think", only to serve a purpose that someone else has defined. We have been loaded up with profound abandonment and profound fear, which gives way to profound anger. However, when we change our way of thinking, we are more able to change our ways of acting. If we can imagine the best self we want to become, we can begin transforming our physical, mental, and spiritual health and habits.

ACT 1.13: WHAT WILL I DO?

What am I willing to do in order to transform my life and become the best self I can be?	
Now:	**Future:**
What is the same?	
What is different?	

What do I commit to now in order to transform my life and become the best self I can be?	
Now:	**Future:**
What is the same?	
What is different?	

THINK: MY LAST LECTURE

I recently gave my last lecture as a teacher education professor and took the opportunity to share some of my learning in the past year about "who I am, what I want, and who I want to become". I share some of that presentation with you in the following paragraphs, as the ideas flow directly from the exercises you have been working with.

"A year ago, I would've easily answered the question 'who are you?' with these and other descriptors: Author; Survivor or Recovering; Soccer, track dad; Border crosser; Partner; Leader; Teacher or professor; Connector. Some of these things are still very true, and there are more today. Some of what I've done academically (related to my service and experiences) has been made public through several academic articles.

Related to university service, I've taken an active role in promoting a field of study (Border Pedagogy) and in encouraging K-12 students, who often remind me of how I suffered silently in middle school or high school. I have sometimes ended the presentation with the words of Winston Churchill: 'never never never quit!' All in all, my work has always kept me active, and sometimes, it's been productive.

Since 2003, when I took up an active role in challenging church leaders and others to take responsibility for their actions that perpetuated child sexual abuse and to work to end child sexual abuse, I have worked hard to find and create ways to bring my whole self to the university. My involvement with the Group Relations Conferences and Border Pedagogy facilitated my integration and restoration. Nonetheless, my Post Traumatic Stress Disorder reached such a level that I needed to take a medical disability leave in the spring of 2006. In the fall, I resumed in the performance of my duties. On the last day of the spring semester of 2007, I received a letter from the provost announcing my non-reappointment for another year, which effectively closed the door to my application for tenure.

At the beginning of this year, I may have said, 'I want to get tenure', or 'I want to get academic recognition for the advocacy work that I have taken up in the past few years.' I might have said that I wanted to expose the corruption in religious or other institutions that lead to child sexual abuse. Or that I wanted to expose the educational practices that hurt people and that lead to the educational disasters that we experience daily.

But the semester has been life-changing for me. I have needed to answer basic questions differently. What I came to realize was that I was like the Jimmy Stewart character in 'It's a Wonderful Life', saying "Please, God. I want to live." Little by little, I noticed the difference in my own capacity to recall and process information, and I have been celebrating little steps in my recovery throughout this year.

I have come to learn some very important lessons in the past several months: That my life is unfolding and made up of pure potentiality (i.e., if I'm be flexible, willing to change, learn, and apply what I learn); that I need to take care of myself before I work effectively with others, especially when there is so much that is abandoning, abusive, or shaming behavior in organizations; that it is more important for me to be happy (with my mind, heart and soul connected) than disconnected and right—the first takes more time. I've learned that peace is possible and difficult, as it requires lots of letting go and re-writing the scripts that have been so familiar for so long. I have learned that I am much more than my titles, or experiences (good and bad), and I am beginning to understand what Marianne Williamson wrote:

> "As we are liberated from our own fear, our presence automatically liberates others."

I have learned that living intentionally requires taking responsibility and discerning. I've learned that what I want is: to end child sexual abuse everywhere. My new title is 'social entrepreneur', which means that I'm a teacher and healer for groups and people who work to transform institutions. What this means in practice is a combination of working with others who intend to end child sexual abuse, writing, and leading seminars."

This process of reconstructing ourselves may not necessarily require us to leave our current work environments or communities in which we live. In fact, I believe that it is only with a solid support base in my home and other spiritual and professional communities that I could make such a large shift in my professional reconstruction. Most significantly, however, was the spiritual development process that helped me to trust my experiences again, re-connect with my physical, emotional, and intellectual vitality. My point in sharing some of my last lecture is that because I have developed a deeper clarity about who I am, I have been able to move forward with a deeper happiness and peace than I ever imagined possible at the beginning of my abuse flashbacks.

SECTION TWO
HOW DOES ABUSE IN RELIGIOUS ENVIRONMENTS HAPPEN?

Victimhood is not an accident or result of individual fault. Victims are created. A long time ago, I bought a then-old Gibson 12-string guitar from a friend for $200.00. At the time, it was a lot of money for me and, while it was beautiful, it never played as well as it could have. I could never tune it as tightly as it should have been, so I adapted by keeping a capo on it. At the time, I loved playing it, however infrequently, but then put in on a shelf in a closet and rarely opened the cheap duct taped case in which it rested. I recently took it off the shelf, and my wife took it to a music store to be re-strung. The person at the music store was shocked that I had such a valuable guitar and that the metal bridge at its base that held the strings in place had been installed backwards. No wonder I couldn't play it right, the way it should have been played all these years. That experience gave me insight into what had happened with me: I was abused and then I continued to play with the misinformation and mal-formation I had for so many years.

THINK: ACCESS AND AUTHORITY

Behind the details of religious authority sexual abuse, the "what", there is a "how". How does abuse happen? In short, abuse happens when there is access and authority. In the case of religious authority child sexual abuse, the authority of imams, gurus, ministers, nuns, priests, rabbis and others is clearly reinforced at individual, family, community and institutional levels. Access, among many things, means an ability to behave in private (as well as in many public places) with a child in ways that could be questioned as socially or emotionally inappropriate. How is it that children are exposed to a variety of influences such as alcohol, pornography, violence or inappropriate social settings that consenting adults may engage in? How is it that a child is allowed, even sent away for the weekend, to be with adults who demonstrate inappropriate interpersonal boundaries or who want to be with children more than family members?

ACT 1.20: AUTHORITY AND ACCESS

Take a few moments to think about how authority was given to your abuser. How was access given to the abuser (i.e., explicit, formal, informal, accidental, etc.)?

THINK: SETTING THE ABUSE STAGE

In my case, my mother considered herself to be a best friend to the pastor who molested me. But before the sexual abuse took place, there was the special attention, the special gifts, and the special trips. Before the sexual abuse took place, the pastor who molested me exposed me to activities with my mother and other adults that included going to bars or having public and private dinners wherein he gave alcohol to me with my mother's consent. My father was physically and emotionally absent or abusive, so the molester priest represented a "good" father figure. Perhaps my mother believed that these were "innocent" exposures to adult settings. In any case, my mother gave the priest who molested me full **access** to me, to take me away from our home and neighborhood, where there might be some responsible adult supervision.

Children, of course, don't give consent to the grooming process or to the actual sexual abuse. Many victims report being sexually illiterate or ambivalent about receiving gifts, participating in secret activities or feeling some level of arousal about what they believe is a solitary experience. Many report being voiceless against physical dominance, verbal abuse, use of life-threatening behaviors, force, sacraments or religious activities by the religious authority to gain control. In various ways, those who abuse children have an informal or formal **authority** that is given to them by family members or caretakers of the child.

ACT 1.21: HOW WAS MY ABUSER GIVEN ACCESS AND AUTHORITY?

Draw or create a collage of words and images from magazines to express your answer to this question. This may take time, and it can serve as a healing exercise in acknowledging your own experience, as well as give you a reference point to which you can compare future reflections upon your safety, health and happiness. This may be an out of workbook activity.

REFLECT: YOUR COLLAGE STORY

Now that you have your collage, step back and let it tell your story: how you began as a beautiful child, what happened to you, and how hard it has been to have lost this childhood beauty and inner life. How will you break your silence or secrecy in a way that helps you maintain your integrity or integrated, connected sense of self?

THINK: AUTHORITY, ACCESS AND SECRECY

The abuser is granted access, meaning time and space, by attentive and caring parents, church or other adult members of community groups who relentlessly believe that no harm could come from the perpetrator. The abuser sometimes takes advantage of a family's or church's state of disarray or dysfunction. When a family or religious group is itself in such a survival mode that it has an authority void, a religious authority appears to be a welcome alternative, a role model, a resource or mentor. Children who grow up emotionally or intellectually starved naturally long for a healthy parent figure. Because religious authorities are so often endowed with the expectation of "holiness", they are a readymade stand-in for the illusory good parent.

A family's or church's need or crisis serves to make what might be seen as questionable behavior or situations that their children experience harder to recognize or address. This was my experience. I carried great shame about my family violence and poverty and then felt even more silenced by my abuser, who told me that what he did was our little secret. Secrecy makes the access and authority that the abuser is given emotionally and spiritually lethal for victims. In my case, the secrecy and silence began before the sexual abuse.

I began to learn that attempts to speak up against abuse were useless before my pastor ever showed up. I have a strong memory about an intervention that my mother attempted with my father's violence in our home related to his alcoholism. It impressed upon me that there was no real mechanism or spoken or unspoken cultural support system that I could rely upon in times of crisis. After many years of fleeing from his rampages or being caught up in his brutal attacks and destruction of our home and whatever was in it, my mother called my father's brother, with whom he had the closest relationship. I was hiding near the conversation outside, where my mother was pleading with my uncle to do something, to get my father to stop, or to help him in some way with his drinking and violence. My uncle said, "You know, *comadre*, when you got married, you said, 'in good times and in bad times.' Call me in the good times. Don't call me in the bad times." And then he left.

ACT 1.22: SCRIPTS OF SILENCE

How were you silenced knowingly or directly with respect to your abuse THEN?

How are you silenced knowingly or directly with respect to current important topics NOW?

What is the same?

What is different?

How did you maintain the secrets surrounding your abuse THEN?

How do you maintain the secrets surrounding your abuse NOW?

What is the same?

What is different?

THINK: CULTURES OF DISBELIEF

Religious authority child sexual abuse is not the fault of the victim. It is not your fault that you were sexually abused as a vulnerable adult by a religious authority. It is not your fault! A terrible analogy of frogs being cooked slowly in a pot of water comes to mind to describe my experience of being groomed and abused by my parish priest and his friend. The story is that scientists sometime, someplace, tested frogs for their survival instincts by putting them in a pot of hot water, and the scientists found that the frogs jumped out immediately. Then the scientists put the frogs into a pot of room temperature water that was slowly heated over time. They found that the frogs' natural instinct to survive was disabled because the environment gradually changed and the discomfort of shock was not there to move them to escape.

How do adults allow child sexual abuse to happen, especially in religious settings? One way of looking at this problem is to say that the adults see what they believe and not the reverse, or believing what they see. In this way, the congregant culture enables the abuse. When adults do not believe what they see, they do not know what they know and effectively know what they are told. Religious authority sexual abuse takes place in environments where congregants are valued for their church or temple membership and obedience more than for their critical or dissenting voices. If adults do not know what they know, how can children understand their own experiences of being abused?

In a church, temple, mosque, etc. culture, children and vulnerable adults become victims of pedophiles who also represent religious or other kinds of authority. The general culture is one of disbelief—no one would ever want to believe that entrusted religious authorities would betray them or rape children. In fact, research shows that when scientists are looking at data with a particular hypothesis in mind, meaning that they have a belief that guides their observations, they actually do not see data that contradicts their expectations (we see what we believe, not believe what we see). In this way, the group enables religious authority abuse to take place by "not knowing what we know". Victims of religious authority sexual abuse have been abused in churches, convents, mosques, rectories, temples, and on school property, as well as in countless places and circumstances away from the official or ceremonial centers. You did not imagine the abuse; others imagined that the abuse was not going on.

The Indian Residential Schools across Canada, however, represent an even more extreme example of the dynamics of abuse of authority and access. In Canada, as in the United States, First Nation or Indian children were forcefully taken from their parents and put into government schools to effectively remove their ethnic identities and assimilate them to the dominant culture. In Canada, the schools were run by religious groups, "so that Indian children could learn Christian morality and work habits away from the influences of the home." (Nicholas F. Davin, Canadian Parliament, 1879). In these settings, not only did the abusers have the access and authority given them by virtue of their religious traditions, but they also had the authority of the state behind them.

Many adults with official authority — teachers, camp counselors, coaches, religious eaders, law-enforcement officers, doctors, judges — are in powerful positions to seduce and manipulate victims and to escape responsibility. Such adults who sexually abuse children are often the most popular teacher, minister, or the best soccer coach. They are sometimes described as "pied pipers" who simply attract children. They are usually believed when they deny any allegations.

ACT 1.23: UNLEARNING HELPLESSNESS, HOPELESSNESS, WORTHLESSNESS

Take a few moments to think about how you learned that you were helpless, powerless or worthless before you were ever physically abused. List ways that adult authority figures communicated to you, directly or indirectly, that you were helpless, powerless, or worthless. For example, do you remember anyone in a position of authority:

	Who	When/ frequency	What did you learn?
Using extreme discipline or punishment on you?			
Spanking or hitting you so hard that you had bruises, cuts, or broken bones?			
Beating or punching you?			
Acting in a way that made you feel powerless?			
Criticizing or making fun of your physical characteristics, such as your hair, your skin color, your body type, or a disability?			

	Who	When/ frequency	What did you learn?
Talking to you in a sexual way, watching you undress or bathe, making you watch pornographic pictures or movies, or photographing you in inappropriate ways?			
Touching you sexually or making you touch yourself or someone else sexually?			
Forcing you to watch or talking you into watching others acting in a sexual way?			
Forcing you to have or talking you into having sex?			
Other:			

REFLECT: ACKNOWLEDGE MIND CONTROL

Religious authority sexual abuse takes place in closed-belief systems. The idea of a closed-belief system is simply that the status quo is maintained, consciously or unconsciously, at any cost. This maintains power, meaning, ideology, and institutional order. In closed-belief systems, dissenting voices are not supported and are sometimes attacked. Often, those who represent something that is contrary to the group ideology and beliefs become "casualties", or people who do not survive the system.

Naming the abuser or circumstance will not bring healing in itself, but it is a start. Take time to acknowledge to yourself the ways you have been infected by the abuse and isolation or secrecy that surrounded it. Your job is to break the isolation and secrecy about such a toxic experience. At this point, perhaps all that might be useful to you is to think about something symbolic you might do with the memories of abuse and isolation that you now have. Perhaps one way to change the isolation or break a toxic secret of abuse in some way that does not bring you or others more abuse is with a trained therapist or with a supportive group of fellow survivors. Others with this particular experience and recovery might be able to share the responses they received from others when they broke their silence about their abuse, as well as what responses have helped them. In any case, they are likely to be supportive and able to hear your story. You may begin to hear with each telling or listening how your story is being re-written to include new interpretations and new chapters in your current life story.

SECTION THREE
WHAT IS THE IMPACT OF ABUSE BY RELIGIOUS AUTHORITIES?

My experience with Religious Authority Sexual Abuse (RASA) shows that it is best understood as a process and not just as an individual event or instances of genital contact. I now understand that RASA is a process that yields patterns of self-destructive lives and lives that are destructive to others. It is no wonder that victims of RASA act as if they were throwing their own lives away. One profound impact of sexual abuse is cognitive. In order to cope with the unspeakable sexual abuse, victims use cognitive coping mechanisms: denial, dissociation, emotional numbing, and repression. This is what I meant in the previous section when I said that children who are sexually abused do not know what they know. This leaves a victim without the ability to describe what has happened. When a person is out of touch with and therefore cannot speak to such profound experiences, she is profoundly **voiceless**.

Each person is different in how she develops resiliency and coping mechanisms related to sexual abuse. However, a child's inability to control what happens to her own body that has been invaded by means of threat or deceit leads to a deep sense of **powerlessness.** Sexual traumatization can be manifested physically as genital trauma, a sign that the victim was without help or **helpless**.

The stigmatization of being sexually abused, especially by a religious authority, often yields a deep sense of shame and guilt of being damaged and bad. Emotionally or sexually, or both, this traumatization can lead to confusion between sex and love, aversion to sex, avoidance of intimacy, and sexual obsessions. I have heard from countless victims that they feel like "damaged goods" at a deep and subconscious level and feel worthless. It is understandable that a victim who cannot ever be good enough or free of a guilt that she does not understand lives with a profound sense of **worthlessness**.

Lastly, a long-term impact of the betrayal by one or more trusted authority figures that sexually abuse children or others who fail to prevent such abuse is mistrust of others, even those close to the victim. Moreover, behind this mistrust of others is the inability of victims to trust their own judgment. It is understandable that a victim who cannot even trust herself lives with a profound insecurity and sense of **hopelessness.**

THINK: SELF-TALK

Earlier, I gave an example about domestic abuse that contributed to my voicelessness, my being unable to reach out to help myself when the sexual abuse from my parish priest began. I had seen that it was futile and humiliating to reach out to others, and that there was no life support, only endurance. My learned helplessness predisposed me to freeze or reach out to no one when I was being sexually abused, or to believe that I was to blame for whatever happened. I learned that I was **not worthy**, that I was **worth less** or worthless.

Victims often develop "voices" that continue to tell us that we are powerless, worthless, helpless or hopeless. Eckhart Tolle gives the following examples of often unconscious (victim) self-talk:

- There is something that needs to happen in my life before I can be at peace, happy, fulfilled, etc. And I resent that it hasn't happened yet. Maybe my resentment will finally make it happen.
- Something happened in the past that should not have happened, and I resent that. If that hadn't happened, I would be at peace now.
- Something is happening now that should not be happening, and it is preventing me from being at peace now.

It is probably no surprise to any victim of RASA

that feeling voiceless, powerless, worthless, and hopeless breeds anger. Growing up, I was an honor student. As a good son and good student, I could never acknowledge the rage that lived and grew in me. I channeled it unknowingly into anything I could that allowed me to win. I recognize now that my academic and athletic performances were driven by a deep and toxic flow of bitterness that translated into competitiveness. I didn't know at the time that that I was expressing hatred for anyone whose life appeared comfortable, like I imagined the priest-abuser's life to be. My anger fueled my competitiveness. I experienced academic success and professional achievement in the field of education, as I repressed memories of sexual abuse by my childhood parish priest and his friend. Perhaps splitting or repressing my own sexual abuse from a conscious level allowed me to manage many other tasks, and perhaps be seen as "driven", or able to manage or control or put out fires.

ACT 1.30: HOW HAS YOUR ANGER SERVED YOU?

How has your anger limited or sabotaged you?	
Then:	**Now:**
What is the same?	
What is different?	

How has your anger served you?	
Then:	**Now:**
What is the same?	
What is different?	

What might be possible in your physical, mental, emotional or spiritual health, or a combination of these, if anger played a much smaller, or at least more appropriate, role in your life?

Then:	Now:

What is the same?

What is different?

REFLECT: IMPACTS OF ABUSE

A)   Take some time to reflect on the impact that abuse has had upon you, in however many ways you can identify. List those things.

B)   Imagine or visualize these various ways that you have been impacted, as if it were one collective image. Draw it.

C)   Give yourself time to grieve whatever pain or rage that comes through your image and this exercise.

THINK: MISPLACED ANGER

For many RASA victims, anger is sometimes misplaced towards authority figures of any sort in destructive ways. It may be an anger that is misdirected towards anyone who shares traits that the abused person identifies with the abuser: gender, status, ideology, etc. Is it any surprise that so many abused children sabotage their own ability to work in systems that require a sense of conformity (e.g., dropping out or feeling "pushed out" from school)?

Given that victims of abuse often feel helpless and voiceless, and believe that their lives are meaningless and purposeless, it makes sense that victims can over-identify in others and find self-worth in helping others. It is difficult to measure the profound insecurity and lack of confidence that victims of abuse often experience, or even to recognize them. Many victims develop strategies to mask these profound insecurities, which is evidence of the resources and resourcefulness that victims develop in order to make sense of their lives and create images of security. Nonetheless, when people's personal boundaries are violated, and I can speak from my own experiences, we develop maladaptive behaviors.

- Stealing from others, whether it be material or emotional;
- Addictive lifestyles (self- or other destructive lifestyles);
- Anti-social behavior that seems like competitiveness or aggressiveness;
- Physical aggression or bullying (abusing others' minds, hearts, or bodies);
- Debating or arguing in order to win;
- Living from crisis to crisis;
- Living to please or to "not make mistakes" as a way to feel loved.

Some victims of abuse misplace anger maybe in becoming disruptive to whatever the larger status quo happens to be. An ongoing impact of abuse may be what seems to be self-inflicted victimization or self-chosen tragic-heroic behaviors that serve others at the victim's cost. In my case, I found myself acting for many years as a kind of Mighty Mouse character, ready at any given moment to protect others from real or symbolic violence.

ACT 1.31: COMMITMENT TO TAKE CARE OF YOURSELF

Your responsibility as a victim is to take care of yourself and commit to having a healthier and more balanced lifestyle. Make a list of all the things that you need to do to have a healthier and more balanced lifestyle. Brainstorm; don't edit.

Physical	
Emotional	
Intellectual	
Spiritual	

Study the list and identify the things that you can do yourself as short or long-term projects. Identify the things that require others' expertise. Share this list with a sponsor or support person (I'll discuss this in the section, "what can you do?") and commit to completing various items on the list.

Physical	Short-term	Long-term
I can do		
Requires others' expertise:		

Emotional	Short-term	Long-term
I can do		
Requires others' expertise:		

Intellectual	Short-term	Long-term
I can do		
Requires others' expertise:		

Spiritual	Short-term	Long-term
I can do		
Requires others' expertise:		

THINK: The Truth May Make You Mad

One axiom we often accept is that the "truth shall set you free." For survivors of RASA, that same truism may seem more like, "the truth may make you mad." Sexual abuse, particularly by a religious authority, is maddening. Consequently, many victims of sexual abuse often develop the following kinds of short-term changes in behavior:

- Overly compliant behavior;
- Acting out or aggressive behavior;
- Acting more mature than we are;
- Persistent or inappropriate sexual play with peers, toys or selves, or sexually aggressive behavior with others;
- Detailed and age-inappropriate understanding of sexual behavior;
- Arriving early at school and leaving late with few, if any absences;
- Poor peer relationships or inability to make friends;
- Lack of trust, particularly with significant others;
- Nonparticipation in school and social activities;
- Inability to concentrate in school;
- Sudden drop in school performance;
- Extraordinary fear of males or females (related to the gender of the perpetrator);
- Seductive behaviors;
- Running away;
- Sleep disturbances;
- Withdrawal;
- Suicidal feelings.

Taking care of ourselves and asking for help are no small tasks for people whose boundaries are such that being vulnerable to others may be extremely threatening or painful. Despite being deeply betrayed by representatives of God, we will need to trust ourselves and others again. Remember that, as victims, we are where we are and, like it or not, we count on others to provide services or counsel that we cannot provide for ourselves at this point.

ACT 1.32: And I love you anyway

At this point, examine the list and note which behaviors have related to you or still relate to you today. If you do not have a safe environment or person to hear you with love, then speak to yourself in the mirror. Take your time "journaling" about these behaviors, recognizing how they have affected you and others.

The following exercise is described as one person speaking to herself. If a support person who is able to participate in this activity without judgment is available, it can be a two-person activity. When you are ready, say and hear the following: First, acknowledge, "I can have _____" (finish the sentence as appropriate from the list above). Be as specific as is helpful for you to hear and recognize the strength of this behavior in your life, or dentify consequences of this behavior to you and others. Second, acknowledge to yourself or have another person acknowledge that this is true, "Yes, you can have that behavior and it does affect you and others." Third, repeat your insight, "I can have ___." Fourth, tell yourself or be told, "Yes, you can _____ AND I love you anyway."

VICTIMS

In this section we have discussed that religious authority sexual abuse happens when there is access and authority given to religious authorities to groom and abuse children and vulnerable adults through what many may have believed were "innocent" exposures to adult settings. Because religious authorities are so often endowed with the expectation of "holiness", they are a ready-made stand-in for the illusory good family, church or community member. This culture of disbelief creates victims. It was not your fault! Your instinct to speak or act was disabled.

Secrecy made the access and authority that the abuser was given emotionally and spiritually lethal. Directly and indirectly a cultural or religious support system failed to protect us and we learned to be silent about the abuse. It is time for you to acknowledge the ways you have been infected by the abuse and secrecy that surrounded it. You are not profoundly voiceless. You are not powerless. You are not worth less or worthless. You are not to blame for whatever happened. Even if you feel like damaged goods, gravely imperfect, you can and must love yourself anyway, the same way other survivors and survivor supporters already do.

Section Four
What can you do?

Where am I going with this? Albert Einstein said, "We can't solve problems by using the same kinds of thinking we used when we created them." I'm not saying that we created our predicament of child sexual abuse, but rather that there's no way to solve a problem of our victimhood with the same mind set that kept us in denial of the problem for so long. There's no way to solve a problem related to our victimhood with the same understanding of ourselves as victims.

I am absolutely not saying that you have created your own problem of victimization by a religious authority. At one point, or for a period of time, when you were voiceless, helpless, and not in a position to intervene and stop the abuse that was happening to you, you got a "victimhood script" to memorize and make your own. Perhaps you got the script from being abandoned and then abused and then ashamed at a profound level that may only now be available for you to understand and let go of. All of that happened in the past. The past is the past.

THINK: New Mind sets

To what degree are your lists or observations about your experiences the same or very similar? Today is yours. Given that we are now dealing with abuse from the past, I am assuming that same abuse by the same abuser is not going on. However, if there are similarities about being dependent, helpless, voiceless, powerless today to what you experienced as a child, then it is absolutely clear, absolutely imperative, and absolutely time for you to transform the mind set of self-images related to victimhood. The practices that flow from this mind set are not helpful in solving today's problems or challenges of living.

It is tricky to deal with the complexity of today's challenges at the same time that we are understanding and letting go of complexities related to our old abuse. This is hard work for anyone. Society, relationships and life are complex and difficult. It is what it is. It will be increasingly complex in the future. The film "Apollo 13" depicted a dilemma that the astronauts had when they didn't have the right equipment to fix a life-threatening mechanical problem. They were literally in a new territory, outer space, in a place that no one could really be prepared for, even if they were very smart, very disciplined, and very committed to working together as a team. I think of their dilemma as a metaphor for victims of religious authority sexual abuse. At one point,

they needed to re-connect their air supply or they would die. We have to reconnect our spiritual air supply or we will die or stay dead, moving and breathing but having no being. The materials the astronauts had, even though they were well-planned and very useful until then, were inadequate to deal with this new and complex problem. The upbringing we had, even though lots of people thought it was beyond reproach, is inadequate to deal with our lives today.

It was absolutely clear, absolutely imperative, and absolutely time for them to let go of all those things that were useful in the past because they were in the present complexity, where blaming or being lost in what could have been, or leaving it up to someone else to do it for them would only lead to their inaction and death. They ended up collectively figuring out how they could put together a solution that helped them to get farther along in their return home, recovery, healthy and alive. It is absolutely clear, absolutely imperative, and absolutely time for us to let go of all those things that were useful in the past because we are in the present complexity, where blaming or being lost in what could have been, or leaving it up to someone else to get healthy for us will only lead to inaction and more death.

VICTIMS

Exercise: Responding to our present predicament

I hope that clarity about your predicament and power will begin to emerge for you. Please answer the following questions:

What is going on in my own thinking and behavior that is related to the past that absolutely needs to change?

What is going on in my present that is being damaged by my dependence on past behaviors or beliefs?

What can I use in my space capsule, and where is my smart support team, that will help me to move forward and live, and become that best person that I will become?

VICTIMS

What can victims who feel helpless or voice-less, or who believe their lives are meaning-less and purposeless, do? On the one hand, there's no one thing, especially anything done in isolation, that a victim can do to be safe, healthy and happy. Religious authority sexual abuse is as much, if not more, of a process than an event, and if the impact of this abuse has been untreated for any amount of time, then recovery is also to be a process.

Living in darkness may be good for fungi, but not for people who wish to transform their feelings of helplessness, voicelessness, meaningless or purposelessness. Victims often feel isolated. One of the maintainers of the deep wounds and disabling trauma is isolation. Therefore, we need to make sure we have a safe environment in which we can share our stories. Support groups can help victims connect with others in a safe environ-ment. Healthy support groups can help those who "don't know what they know" about abuse to "know what we don't know" about recovery: being safe, healthy, and happy. Healthy support groups can help victims develop voice, find meaning, and learn to help themselves in their recovery. The following quote comes from support literature related to those who have survived RASA.

> No matter how old we are when the memories of our abuse return, the revelation of the reality of what happened to us is so shattering, that in the initial stages of our healing most of us are incapacitated by PTSD (Post Traumatic Stress Disorder). Recovery is a gradual process and a painfully dif-ficult one, but it is not insurmountable. It is made worse by having to do it alone. Some of us, but not all, from time to time have at least one person who walks with us a while, and that person makes all the difference. But it is not enough. We need each other and the community we are building.

Knowledgeable therapists and other professionals along with friends can provide us support, but they have not been on the inside of ritualized trauma experiences as we have. No one can provide the validation and healing container that we find in each other's company.

Various forms of 12-step recovery, even if they are not directly about recovery from religious authority or other sexual abuse, may be very valuable in helping a person to learn from others and have a safe space in which to share our struggles in recovery. Many survivors have a very difficult time in 12-step groups because of the use of "God" in some form. Many have found ways to adjust the images or meanings of the word "God". One is: "Good Orderly Direction". No group or therapist is perfect. However, recovering by oneself from a social, interpersonal betrayal and violation that damages emotional and spiritual boundaries is not an option. Hope-lessness may live in isolation, but hope grows in a supportive group setting.

By participating in such groups, working with a trained therapist, as well as by writing about our own experiences, we practice developing a voice. This process may begin by merely being in the company of others who are in active recovery, listening to and learning from their stories. It may be that the process of developing our own voice about our abuse and healing begins with limited, halting speech about our abuse. Reading others' stories and formal research about abuse, impact, and recovery sometimes helps people develop their own voice. These actions help us develop our voices, which can eventu-ally be used in positive ways to help others. See chapter 6 for books and films that relate to healing from various kinds of trauma and betrayal.

VICTIMS

Go back and repeat the process that you have just practiced, with one aspect of who you are with another aspect of who you are. Compare the insight you have gathered from that reflection to the insight from your first exercise. Look for some common themes that may be addressed by one change of behavior or change of thinking. You can revisit any of these exercises at any point. Meanwhile, I encourage you to do something today that is good for you. In our analogy of the

CALENDAR

	SUNDAY	MONDAY	TUESDAY
PHYSICAL			
EMOTIONAL			
INTELLECTUAL			
SPIRITUAL			

post-accident emergency room, make sure that you are getting oxygen or vital life support, whether that be physical, mental, or spiritual.

Go back and look at the lists you created on pages 35-36. Choose something that will help you have an improved state of physical, mental, emotional, or spiritual health and do it. You deserve to be cared for well.

WEDNESDAY	THURDAY	FRIDAY	SATURDAY

VICTIMS

The purpose or job of a person in the throes of feeling the impact of abuse is to take care of ourselves. That may mean exercising, or a change of diet or lifestyle towards better health and balance. It may mean that we give ourselves positive examples of surviving trauma and challenges by watching inspiring movies or listening to beautiful music. It may mean that we take time every day to practice paying attention to our living environment and to take note of what we need to do in order to have a healthier living environment.

The most consistent and repeated message instilled in us by our offenders is that of "don't tell." Therefore, it is very important that we do tell—that we tell ourselves, each other, and to the extent that each individual is capable, the greater community. It is in telling our stories that we reclaim and proclaim who we are, that we break down the bonds of programming. The more trauma and fear are replaced with the truth of our experiences, and witnessed by the human community, the freer we become.

Although our spirits may have been injured, they were not captured. Each human spirit belongs only to that person and his or her Creator, however the person perceives that Creator, and is part of an undamaged core that can never be defiled. Healing is a process that emanates from that core. We believe that it is the essence of humanity to be hard wired to heal, and that healing begins the instant injury

occurs. So while healing is not given to us by others, it can be facilitated by the skilled and loving witness of others.

Finally, it is time to make a tentative plan. Given our growing clarity about who we are, where we are, who we are working with, what we are willing to do, what we see that we do not want, and what we see that we do want, we can begin to make a plan for ourselves. It is challenging that we all are learning as we move forward. We are learning to make our own decisions from a vision of health and in a process that address some of the complexity of religious authority sexual abuse. We are learning to question the utility of our own conclusions about our resources, ourselves and those around us.

Our best plan today is tentative because, as we practice new behaviors towards recovery, health, and happiness, we will change and others will change what we currently know. Our recovery is not going to be a dance of certainty and control, which is no dance at all, nor will it be a free-for-all interpretation of whatever in the moments we feel inspired to do in the name of recovery. This beginning structure or plan for our health and happiness reflects new thinking, and all that old learning and behaving will resist or push against our plan, but it won't negate or destroy our plan. We may need to make adjustments after we have tested, reflected and concluded that we have learned something.

ACT 1.42: BOUNDARIES

Taking care of ourselves and asking for help are no small tasks for people whose boundaries are such that being vulnerable to others may be extremely threatening or painful. Our boundaries have been profoundly impacted, if not infected or shattered in ways that we never knew, as we continued to do our best after the abuse. We will have healthy boundaries that are flexible, that help us to understand who we are and to transform who we are — that clarify for ourselves and for others who we are. Whether or not anyone has suffered the abuse that you have suffered, managing healthy boundaries is difficult work and we all need healthy boundaries.

What are these boundaries that have been disintegrated through our physical, emotional, psychological and spiritual abuse by a religious authority? They are appropriate limits that help us maintain our integrity, or integrated, connected sense of self. They are particularly important for those of us who have had our physical, intellectual, emotional, and spiritual boundaries violated by a representative of God, a person who held a higher authoritative rank than members of our family, church and community and a person who often managed the boundaries of our family, church, or community.

Personal boundaries that are too closed, inflexible or rigid, lead to irreconcilable differences in relationships or working with others. They reflect a disconnection from others. Personal boundaries that are too open make it so that we don't know where we end and another begins, often resulting in being too intrusive or being intruded upon. In other words, we are overly dependent on others to have a sense of who we are. Permeable boundaries are healthy: like a healthy cell membrane that keeps a cell intact so that it can develop as it is meant to on its own, and also can take in what is useful from the environment. Cells with permeable boundaries can join purposefully with another cell when appropriate.

This activity is to help clarify the importance of developing healthy boundaries for ourselves. I consider some of the behaviors that victims of religious authority sexual abuse develop at the time of the abuse according to the following areas, as a way to see how pervasive the impact of RASA can be upon a victim. Check off the ones that you identify with and consider for yourself how your boundaries related to these areas have been too open or too closed, and how you have grown since then.

Behavior	YES	NO	Area of/ for growth
Stealing, whether it be material or emotional			
Addiction (self or other destructive lifestyles)			
Anti-social behavior that seem like competitiveness or aggressiveness			
Physical aggression or bullying (abusing others' minds, hearts, or bodies)			
Debating or arguing in order to win			
Living from crisis to crisis			

Behavior	YES	NO	Area of/ for growth
Living to please or "not make mistakes" as a way to feel loved			
Overly compliant behavior			
Acting out or sexually aggressive behavior			
Acting more mature than we are			
Persistent and/ or inappropriate sexual play with peers, toys or selves			
Detailed and age-inappropriate understanding of sexual behavior			
Arriving early at school and leaving late with few, if any absences			
Poor peer relationships or inability to make friends			
Lack of trust, particularly with significant others			
Nonparticipation in school and social activities			
Inability to concentrate in school			
Sudden drop in school performance			

Behavior	YES	NO	Area of/ for growth
Extraordinary fear of others (related to the gender of the perpetrator)			
Seductive behaviors			
Running away			
Sleep disturbances			
Withdrawal			
Suicidal feelings			

THINK: FINAL THOUGHTS

When I was a child, I spent a great amount of time with my maternal grandmother, who was blind. She wore dark glasses at all times. Because she could navigate from room to room and function on her own in so many ways, cooking, washing dishes, dressing herself, etc., I believed that she was only pretending to be blind. I sometimes waited to see if she would not know that I was in the room and would take off her glasses and look around with her completely functional eyes. And one day, she did take off her opaque glasses, only to reveal white pupils that could not see.

As the Boston reports of abuse came forward, I was barraged by flashbacks and anxiety attacks. I longed for a shred of the comfort that I had known in my past religious traditions, to which I had devoted years of my identity, purpose, and desire to serve soci-

ety. Think about this: The comfort that you found from your past religious traditions also made you completely vulnerable to being sexually and spiritually violated. For too long, I continued to believe that there was something wrong with me, whether at conscious or subconscious levels. I continued to maintain a child-like expectation that somehow, someone else would do something that would make a difference in what I had lost. I was blind to what I did not want to see: that I was searching and longing for healing from the wrong authority or from someone who was blind to my experience.

When I understood how I had been victimized, I spoke up. My rage compelled me to protect others from similar pain and spiritual death. I protested by handing out leaflets to let parishioners know about the history of child sexual abuse in their parish, about the practice of deceit and organized campaigns of public relations efforts to minimize attention on past and present sexual abuse by religious authorities. Somewhere between the rejection and hostility of parishioners who faced me alongside this tribute of leaflets and spoke to reporters in front of diocesan offices or cathedrals and when I moved to another church, and then another, I began to see the reality of my spiritual death. I began to see what I referred to in the introduction, that I now knew what I didn't know. Religious authority sexual abuse is possible when pedophiles are given authority by others, who are responsible for protecting children, access to the victims, and can maintain a level of secrecy about their behavior in a religious community.

This chapter is essentially an acknowledgement of the past victimization and trauma that has come to those sexually abused as children. As difficult as it may be to acknowledge what has happened and how we have lived as victims, it is an essential step towards healing. The past is the past, yet victims continue to be impacted, often without consciousness of the past as it operates in the present. This chapter recognizes that we have been conditioned to not think, only to serve a purpose that someone else has defined.

In this stage of your recovery, I encourage you to be the recipients of care. If we use the analogy of the aftermath of a life-threatening accident, you might need to receive blood or an organ transplant. Your first job as an adult who is coming to terms with having been sexually abused by a religious authority is to take care of yourself and to commit to having a healthier and more balanced lifestyle. You are worth it.

Victims of child sexual abuse have experienced profound damage to their personal boundaries, self worth, and perception of the world. After some mourning of the past, you may come to accept that the past is the past. The spiritual tools that you used or relied upon in the past are past. Today begins the difficult work of reconciling our past with our present and living in the present. I wish you steady healing and wisdom from the community of survivors of religious authority sexual abuse.

ACT 1.43: THEN AND NOW

Behavior:	
Then:	**Now:**
What is the same?	
What is different?	
What do I commit to now in order to transform my life and become the best self I can be?	

Behavior:	
Then:	**Now:**

What is the same?

What is different?

What do I commit to now in order to transform my life and become the best self I can be?

REFLECT: YOU ARE NOT ALONE

Congratulations on the work you have done in this chapter. Spiritually, victims have often been absent or asleep. There is a metaphor about breathing that victims have inhaled and have held it in for a lifetime. The damage done to victims' boundaries and sense of self through Religious Authority Sexual Abuse is immeasurable. Your job now is to stop and get help. By doing so, you will begin to separate your best self from the voices in our heads that say:

"There is something that needs to happen in my life before I can be at peace, happy, fulfilled, etc. And I resent that it hasn't happened yet. Maybe my resentment will finally make it happen."

"Something happened in the past that should not have happened, and I resent that. If that hadn't happened, I would be at peace now."

"Something is happening now that should not be happening, and it is preventing me from being at peace now."

The initial victim experience may leave us feeling like a child that cries because our toy — religion, which represents our spirit — has been taken away. We may be resentful or angry that someone else seems to have more than we do of our toy. Our critical thinking may be low in this state of mind. However, we have been conditioned to not think, only to serve a purpose that someone else has defined. In addition, we have been loaded up with "primordial abandonment", and "primordial fear" as a result of RASA, which gives way to "primordial anger". You are not alone, and this fear or anger will not last, although you have work to do. Welcome to the work that will lead you to freedom and a spiritual life that you may not believe is possible at this time.

Share your thoughts on this book & possibly win prizes.
Everyone who shares ideas on how to make this workbook better
will get a free copy of the next edition of the book.
Go to www.HTSAH.com or www.HealingTheSexuallyAbusedHeart.com

CHAPTER TWO
SURVIVORS

INTRODUCTION

Chapter 2 is about self-victimization. In the movie "The Love Guru", Mike Myers holds up one of his many books, entitled, *Stop hitting yourself! Stop hitting yourself! Why are you still hitting yourself?* This chapter is about helping survivors to stop hitting ourselves. Stop kidding yourself. Stop cheating yourself. Stop seeing yourself as worthless. Stop pretending to yourself. Stop ignoring yourself. Stop lying to yourself.

On the other hand, this chapter is about helping survivors to start some new behaviors. Start attending to yourself. Start being honest with yourself. Start seeing yourself as worthy of love and healthy relationships. Start seeing yourself as your true self. I ended chapter 1 with the admonition or well-intended suggestion to "take care of yourself". Just so you don't think I am either a complete idiot or out of touch with what it means to recover, I want to say a bit more about what I mean by "yourself". Let's start with "self". What self?

While religious people or teachings may have told us that we are children of God, the powerful actions by religious authorities told us even more loudly that we were our experiences of abuse. As a result of being sexually abused by people who we perceived to be of God, our self was damaged, if not practically extinguished from us. We were left with our experiences of abuse, which we could not acknowledge, but which became confused with our "self". However we managed our ways through life, we were probably not conscious of how or how much we accepted a script that told us we were worthy of abuse. As a result, many victims,

good, smart, generous, talented, and beautiful people, have become self-sacrificing, self-sabotaging, self-selling, self-distracting, or otherwise self-loathing. A survival mechanism that many of us practiced was inventing ourselves, in large part by who we thought others wanted us to be, without really knowing who we are.

When many people become conscious of the abuse or the effects of the abuse, it can be like a slap that jolts a newborn into sudden independent, albeit painful, breathing. At a spiritual level, I see victims as symbolically holding in a multi-year breath that contains the secrets of the abuse. Survivors, on the other hand, emotionally exhale and are caught up in the trauma and drama of breathing out the toxic shame and rage that we have held on to for so long. Neither holding it all in nor letting it all out is healthy in itself. In time and with intention, our breathing will become manageable and even powerful. For the time being, the experiences related to finding our voice and learning how to manage it let us know that there is a self that wants to be and breathe normally.

The ways we think or talk about RASA go beyond an involuntary holding it in, or not talking about the abuse, or talking about the abuse that happened to us as though it is the only truth we know. Eckhart Tolle gives the following examples that relate to the thinking or beliefs that Survivors often use unconsciously as self-talk:

"Nobody respects and appreciates me. I need to fight to survive. There is never enough money.

Life always lets you down. I don't deserve abundance. I don't deserve love."

"You should do this or that so I can be at peace. And I resent that you haven't done it yet. Maybe my resentment will make you do it."

"Something you (or I) did, said, or failed to do in the past is preventing me from being at peace now."

"What you are doing or failing to do now is preventing me from being at peace."

One goal of this chapter is to help you to see your own experiences and subsequent unhealthy thought processes and behaviors as something that you're sick of and that do not serve you well. A spiritual hope in this chapter is that you will recognize and dissolve some of your many illusions that have kept you focused on the past and future, so that you have been unable to enjoy the present moment or the presence in and around yourself, which is the beginning of healing and transcendence.

THINK: OUR AUTOBIOGRAPHY

I wrote the following in a poem called "Settled", several years ago, when I first read about a legal settlement for victims of clergy sexual abuse. As I look at it now, I see that it reflects what I am describing as survivor self-talk.

Settled
Like silt lining a pond or pieces of the Titanic at
the bottom of the icy ocean.
DNA Catholics don't see settlement terms as
the floating wreckage of our lives, but as an
oil spill that we caused, polluting their mother
church, not mine, no more
Smother mothering, abusive mothering,
dependent on the tit mothering
I love them and hate them, authority figures,
people in positions of power,
Who offer life preservers to one another while I
sink

After a tornado, some homes are found miles
away, others devastated and others
not touched at all.
My phantom life is strewn across the
countryside with the bodies of others
Monsignor Perp destroyed
unchecked, awed, while faithful Catholics saw
what they believed.

I run unceasingly, barefoot, looking for my
resurrected soul
Carrying an anchor, long separated from the
connecting chains called faith

I didn't lose my faith,
It died a painful, slow death from internal
bleeding that clergy addicted Catholics would
not see

At first, I carried on as if it had just gone out of
town for a retreat and would come back any
minute and we'd be a happy couple again,
made for each other,
A match made in heaven, or hell.
It's all mixed up, like me, in my in-between
church where
I received Eucharist from a woman priest,
but not the smiling, round, White bishop in his
crimson and lace dress.

Now I sit holding my dead soul like an anchor,
like the Pieta,
As if by loving it enough, it would come back to
life.
It would take an act of God,
Who fell asleep at the helm, letting the ship of
my life be gouged by an ordained iceberg
And settle at the bottom of the sea

Consider *Autobiography in five short chapters,* by Portia Nelson. In chapter one, she describes walking down a street and falling into a deep hole in the sidewalk. She's lost and helpless, and it takes forever to find a way out. In chapter two, she walks down the same street with the same deep hole in the sidewalk. She pretends she doesn't see it and falls in again.

She is somehow surprised that she is in the same place. Again, she thinks it isn't her fault and again it takes her a long time to get out. In chapter three, she walks down the same street, sees the hole, and falls in anyway because it is a habit. She takes responsibility for herself and gets out immediately. In chapter four, she walks down the same street and walks around the hole in the sidewalk. In chapter five, she walks down another street.

In this story, the first three chapters speak to the illusions that keep us from the reality or moment at hand. Like the poem "Settled", it speaks to survivors' expressions of feeling profoundly let down. It expresses resentment and holds a thinly veiled expectation that our resentment will bring about change. It makes others' actions or inactions responsible for our lack of presence. I mean this in a descriptive way, not as a way of shaming or disparaging myself or other survivors. The poem expressed my deep feelings and experiences in that part of my recovery at that time.

ACT 2.00: KNOWING THAT YOU KNOW

Take some time to think of how these self-talk or "life in five chapters" descriptions fit with your experience, now that you are an adult. Re-consider how your experiences of abuse relate to the answers you gave in response to the question, "Who are you?" If you completed the exercise in chapter 1 to write, draw, paint, or express in whatever creative way you could how those past experiences impacted your identity or sense of self, look at that creative expression. This may be an out-of-workbook activity.

REFLECT: SELF TALK

Consider how the self-talk examples relate to what you expressed and how they may have influenced your sense of self. Now you know that you know, and you can begin to see a deeper, best self that is different from the self-talk self you have worked with for so long.

THINK: RE-WRITING SCRIPTS

Chapter 1 described the person who was a victim, who didn't know any better. Bad things have happened to us. This chapter describes those of us who live at a level of survival, who in many ways perpetuate our own trauma, either by pretending that we don't see the hole in the sidewalk, or by knowing what is there and falling in anyway. These following exercises are intended to help you re-write the scripts you currently have so that they become scripts of self-care, health, and happiness, or walking down another street. Is this an overly ambitious goal, some phony promise, some shell game of recovery that promises one thing and leads to nothing? If you're asking those questions, keep reading and see what happens. What have you got to lose but the old scripts and behaviors that don't serve you, that don't help you shine, that keep you in fear and insecurity?

ACT 2.01: BREATHING AFFIRMATIONS

We have breathed in the smog of self-worthlessness. We have absorbed messages that are abusive, thoughtless, and untrue about ourselves. We need to breathe in pure oxygen about who we are. Borrowing from the analogy of being in an emergency room, a post-operation room or even an intensive care unit, survivors are those patients who need to be breathing in pure oxygen and receiving in this stage of healing. It is not a failing or unreasonable demand on our part that we need pure oxygen or particular nourishment as part of our recovery.

What is this pure oxygen? Affirming your goodness. Focusing on pure affirmations is a useful practice that assists in your healing process. This exercise is intended to help you enrich and stabilize your breathing, or way of thinking, about your experiences, relationships, and yourself, so you can move on to other levels of emotional and spiritual healing. Take several minutes to let each of the following affirmations sink into your consciousness of who and what you are.

Sit comfortably with your spine upright. Close your eyes and visualize a deep center of your very self within you. Take a deep breath and on the inhalation, let the first word rise into your mind; exhale and let the idea drop with your breath into your core. Repeat this process slowly, breathing deeply and naturally, letting each word filter from your mind to your inner core.

> *beautiful,*
> *brilliant,*
> *talented,*
> *free to be curious,*
> *a spiritual being having a human experience,*
> *a gentle soul,*
> *a gift from God,*
> *a spark of God,*
> *pure consciousness,*
> *a manifestation of spirit*

REFLECT: PRACTICAL MEDITATION

Notice how you feel in this kind of meditation. Practice this informally when walking throughout the day, or if you can, practice while you are doing something repetitive that doesn't take much attention. Notice how the practice affects you throughout the day.

When you control a man's thinking, you do not have to worry about his actions. You do not have to tell him not to stand here or go yonder. He will find his 'proper place' and will stay in it. You do not need to send him to the back door. He will go without being told. In fact, if there is no back door, he will cut one for his special benefit. His education makes it necessary.

-Dr. Carter G. Woodson

Dr. Carter G. Woodson, a distinguished author, editor, publisher, and historian, is called the "father of Black history". He believed that Blacks should know their past in order to participate effectively in society today. He believed that Black history, which many tried diligently to erase, was very important for Blacks to build upon in order to be productive members of society.

I believe that there is a social parallel for survivors who are beginning to bring an important history, one which many people would rather not have come forward, to light. I believe that there is a psychic parallel for survivors who continue to "choose the back door" of dignity, self-worth, health and happiness, even when it appears that there is nothing holding us back. I believe that survivors must acknowledge that we have come to believe or act as if our proper place is to be invisible, unworthy, or disconnected from ourselves and others, in order for us to become healthy and happy. Review the story of recovery in five stages, depicted by Portia Nelson. What is the hole in the sidewalk that you repeatedly fall into? How do you pretend that the hole is not there?

The following exercise can help you think or act purely or with a commitment to your best self. When we act purely, we're focused and we don't get lost in distractions from our focus. We also recognize old patterns of belief and behavior as old patterns that do not help us in taking care of ourselves.

ACT 2.02: THINKING PURELY

Take any one of your answers you came up with to the "who are you?" exercises in chapter 1, and answer the following questions with that in mind. Identify behaviors that you can demonstrate now and in a year or more from now. Then jot down some particular physical, emotional, intellectual or spiritual practices that could support your vision now and in the future. If it helps, include answers that you may not believe about yourself, but that others have pointed out about you. If this exercise is particularly difficult, go back to the beginning of the chapter and see if any of the self-talk examples are getting in the way of completing these answers. If that is the case, you now know that you know and can answer with the freedom of knowing that you are becoming familiar with your best self.

How would I and others benefit if I acted purely as ___?

Now:	Future:

Physical

Emotional

Intellectual

Spiritual

What do I need in order to be able to act purely as ____?

Now:	Future:

Physical

Emotional

Intellectual

Spiritual

What do I mean by living at a level of survival? I mean acting as if there are no choices. For some people, that may lead to living at a subsistence level. For others, it may mean acting as if there are no choices amid plentiful resources, financial and other. In many situations, it is living with a mindset of "either-or" thinking. In some cases, this thinking may be fairly simplistic or silly, as illustrated in the following example.

I recently took my sons to a beach house and after a great day of swimming and eating up the great food and sounds of the waves, the boys fell asleep in the living room. They began being harassed by mosquitoes, unbeknownst to me. I was bothered by some mosquitoes as well, but not enough to get out of bed and put on some Skin so Soft as a mosquito repellant. When I woke up, the boys were gone. I figured that they were out taking a walk. After a few minutes, I found a note that said, "We're in the car. We have the keys."

Later, when I talked with them, I found out that they hadn't been able to bear the mosquitoes. I realized that one window without a screen had been left open and that the mosquitoes had come from outside, not inside the house. However, their either-or thinking had been that they either stay inside and suffer or go to the car. Another part of their survival thinking was "as if": They go to the car, they'll be better off because the mosquitoes must be coming from inside the house.

They moved out to the car and spent an uncomfortable few hours. They learned that by leaving the windows slightly open, the car filled up with mosquitoes, and so they had to roll up the windows. Another part of survival thinking, as if there are no choices, became clear when my son came in from the car and said, "I wish we had had some Skin So Soft last night." He knew that it had helped repel bugs from several previous camping trips. I said, "We do." He hadn't known and had acted as if we had had none.

We laughed later about the dilemma they had faced while they were sealed up in the car: breathing or bleeding. The car became a sauna of their sweat in the seats and their breath condensed on every centimeter of the windows. Some survival thinking can be silly.

The survivor thinking and behavior described in this chapter is much more serious because it stems from experiences of molest that are followed by acting as if nothing of consequence has happened. *Crosses: Survivors of Clergy Sexual Abuse* gives many examples of survivors' experiences, a child being molested by a religious authority in school, in a church setting, and then returning to class, or in the victim's home and then returning to be with others and being expected to function as if nothing had happened. Such experiences illustrate another immeasurable impact on other victims who witness their friend return and who feel shame and sorrow for their friend, as well as guilty relief that they were spared this time.

We did not create the abuse or the dynamics that led to and perpetuated our abuse. It may have served us somehow in the past to repress the memories or act as if the abuse or the dynamics that led to our abuse did not exist. However, it is time for us to practice a new set of understandings, beliefs and behaviors. It is time to understand how you contribute to your own contemporary victimization. Take time to say the following to yourself and to let it sink into your consciousness:

I have been a victim who didn't know any better. I am not a victim any longer.

I will no longer perpetuate my own trauma.

I did not create the abuse or the dynamic through which I was abused; I will no longer pretend that this dynamic was or is not in place around me.

How am I keeping myself from living more fully or meaningfully as _____?

Now:	Future:

Physical

Emotional

Intellectual

Spiritual

SURVIVORS

What experiences or affirmations tell me in some way that I am acting positively as _____?

Now:	Future:

Physical

Emotional

Intellectual

Spiritual

SURVIVORS

Chapter 1's focus was mourning our past. In this chapter, we continue to build on the foundational question, "Who are you?" as we focus on the stage of recovery that I describe as mourning our present. This mourning process can move us to further reconcile and later re-integrate the profound disintegration in our bodies, minds, hearts, and souls related to RASA. This mourning process can help us to think critically about who we are, and to see ways that we have perpetuated our own unhappiness or poor health. My goal in this chapter is to help you further understand and appreciate ways we've internalized abuse, and to imagine and begin to integrate a new vision of yourself. The first sets of exercises are intended to help you believe that you are worth having a healthier and more balanced lifestyle.

Your job as a survivor is to recognize ways that you currently contribute to victimizing yourself and to take concrete steps to change such behavior. You are worth it. That's all.

SECTION ONE
WHAT DOES IT MEAN TO BE A 'SURVIVOR?'

THINK: NO LONGER VICTIMS

Identifying as a survivor indicates to oneself and to others that we are now conscious of the abuse and are no longer willing to live as victims of it. While our literal sexual victimization happened and continues to impact us, we are no longer victims. Therefore, the terminology we use to describe ourselves is significant.

Another aspect of the term "survivor" is literal. The truth is that many victims of religious authority sexual abuse have taken their lives. The term, therefore, describes a person who has lived with sexual abused by a religious authority figure or who has survived "failed" suicide attempts.

Physical scars help us remember what happened, without causing the physical pain that created the scar. RASA survivors often suffer internal and spiritual pain that is not obvious to a passerby. It is a private pain that many live with or "survive", as if it's just the way life is. The following is a partial list of what survivors privately struggle with as they become conscious of their religious authority sexual abuse. They are some of the symptoms of Post-Traumatic Stress Disorder. RASA survivors can:

Have flashbacks of the abuse;
Have frequent nightmares;
Be sensitive to noise, being touched, or being close to people;
Always expect something bad to happen;
Become angry easily;
Not remember periods of their lives;
Feel numb;
Let people abuse or take advantage of them;
Abuse others;
Feel depressed, even suicidal.

ACT 2.10: RASA SURVIVOR IDENTIFICATION

Dr. Janet G. Woititz identified the following list of behaviors related to adult children of alcoholics. However, given the fact that RASA victims have had a profound trauma to our boundaries and sense of self —our soul — it is no surprise that many RASA survivors can also identify with these symptoms of spiritual devastation. I have substituted "RASA survivors" for "adult children", and have put them into a grid, so you can consider to what degree they have related to you and how they relate to you now. Choose a period of time, for example, a decade, or a point in time, for example, five years ago or when you first acknowledged your abuse to another person, and compare your answers to today.

RASA survivors:

...have difficulty in following a project through from beginning to end. THEN	Very true	Somewhat true	Slightly true
NOW			
...lie when it would be just as easy to tell the truth. THEN	Very true	Somewhat true	Slightly true
NOW			

		Very true	Somewhat true	Slightly true
...judge themselves without mercy.	THEN	Very true	Somewhat true	Slightly true
	NOW			
...guess at what normal is.	THEN	Very true	Somewhat true	Slightly true
	NOW			
...have difficulty having fun.	THEN	Very true	Somewhat true	Slightly true
	NOW			
...take themselves very seriously.	THEN	Very true	Somewhat true	Slightly true
	NOW			
...have difficulty with intimacy.	THEN	Very true	Somewhat true	Slightly true
	NOW			
...overreact to changes over which they have no control. THEN		Very true	Somewhat true	Slightly true
	NOW			
...constantly seek approval/affirmation. THEN		Very true	Somewhat true	Slightly true
	NOW			
...feel they are different than others.	THEN	Very true	Somewhat true	Slightly true
	NOW			
...are either super responsible or super irresponsible. THEN		Very true	Somewhat true	Slightly true
	NOW			
...are extremely loyal, even in the face of evidence that loyalty is undeserved. THEN		Very true	Somewhat true	Slightly true
	NOW			
...tend to lock themselves into a course of action without giving serious consideration to alternative behaviors or possible consequences. THEN		Very true	Somewhat true	Slightly true
	NOW			

REFLECT: AFFIRMATIONS

Go back to the list of affirmations and repeat some of your own affirmations, given your experiences with this exercise. I am flexible in my thinking; I approve of myself; I love myself without limits; etc.

Damaged goods, not right, f*d up by God's messenger. Those are some of the shameful thoughts about ourselves that survivors carry. Shame is the stuff of our spiritual cancer that has infected us and has been festering in us despite —or even as motivation for— our best efforts to help others and make the world better for others. This spiritual cancer is what some victims do not survive. Consider the story of you waking up in the spiritual intensive care unit and finding out that you have been diagnosed with spiritual cancer, which is even more painful than physical cancer. You have it and you need treatment now. This condition is behind the various symptoms of emotional or spiritual disease, the being uncomfortable with our own souls, listed in the previous two pages.

This condition has landed you where you are now, waking up from the abuse as an adult. When a person is hospitalized and recovering from a significant health intervention, that person has a particular selection of foods, medicines and therapies that are helpful to nurture her system forward in the healing process. Some of the nourishment may even be given to the patient without her knowing exactly how it serves a particular purpose at this particular time. Spiritually, the experience might be as if we were dreaming, out of control of what is going on around us, and not making sense of much of what is happening.

Is it any wonder that we survivors are not always easy people to deal with? Okay, we are often not easy people to deal with, and, unfortunately, we don't usually know it. Who has time or energy to be appreciative of other people's gestures of kindness or thoughtfulness when we are in the middle of our own trauma? How in the world can anyone who is witnessing her own festering emotional, spiritual, or intellectual wounds erupt in and around her think about what other people might be going through? These are descriptive questions, not judgments or indictments.

However, recovery requires working with, despite, and through our own woundedness and recognizing others' gifts and suffering. As painful as it has been for me to look honestly at the magnitude of the damages I endured through abandonment, sexual abuse and shame that came from the abuse, it was at least that difficult for me to recognize the ways that I have unknowingly abandoned, neglected, abused, or shamed others. This moment of recognition is not the only point at which a survivor can tap into a kind of generosity, kindness, or even interest towards others. It was, nonetheless, an important turning point for me.

What it means to be a survivor is to go through the process of stepping back into our own lives, our own bodies, and our own hearts. It can be a very painful process; we have stayed away for a long time for that very reason. What is different about this moment in time, I believe, is that we have hit bottom, the ground floor of our pain and illusions that helped us to look away from the pain. Congratulations. Yes, congratulations. You have nowhere to go but up—if you really want up, if you've suffered enough. The rest of this chapter will help you clarify if you've really done your time and are willing to open a door and let yourself out of the prison that you've been in for so long.

ACT 2.11: THEN AND NOW CONTEXTS

You have begun to clarify who you are and who you want to become. This gives an essential direction or perhaps vision beyond our current experience. The following exercise is intended to help you clarify connections to the past which seem to be related or grounded in your functioning as an adult. Answer the following questions in a few words and try to identify what is different about the ways you grew up and the ways you now live: physically, financially, geographically, socially, emotionally, intellectually, spiritually, etc.

What was your neighborhood like growing up and what is your neighborhood like now? What was your financial security or stability like growing up and how is it now?	
Then:	**Now:**
What is the same?	
What is different?	
What do you want for yourself in this area?	

How did or do you feel about where you lived growing up and where you live now?	
Then:	**Now:**
What is the same?	
What is different?	
What do you want for yourself in this area?	

What were your intimate relationships like growing up and what are your love life or intimate relationships like now?

Then:	Now:

What is the same?

What is different?

What do you want for yourself in this area?

How did you understand and solve problems growing up and how do you understand and solve problems now?

Then:	Now:

What is the same?

What is different?

What do you want for yourself in this area?

THINK: LIVE IN THE MOMENT

I know it can be very difficult for survivors to be present to ourselves and to our needs and desires. Here's an example of what I mean by how important and perhaps difficult it is to be able to respond to or for ourselves in the present. I took a white water rafting trip with my family about a year and a half ago as a way to celebrate new behaviors and changes in my life. At one point, I took the opportunity to jump out of the raft and float through some rapids. I knew it would be challenging, exciting and exhilarating. But I did not anticipate the shock of the cold water that made it difficult to breathe. Within seconds, I was speeding feet first into the rapids, water shooting into my mouth and nose, and I was struggling to breathe. The guide and raft were always in sight, and I thought that I would drown. Despite my experience, I had to force myself to wave and shout that I needed help. Within seconds, another raft floated by and the guide asked if I was okay. I was just out of the worst of the rapids and able to lean back, breathe and float. Instead of taking an oar or hand and getting help, I made a joke about drinking water. Even in the face of present danger, I struggled against seeking help because I had a powerful shame reaction to being needy, vulnerable, or in distress.

It is very possible that you have been doing an amazing job of helping others in many ways while neglecting yourself. In that case, do not underestimate the power of being able to ask for or accept help when it is offered to you in small ways. Before we can give in ways that do not do harm to ourselves, we must receive. For us to receive, we must be present.

In a sense, before we can give or live fully from our best self, we must receive the present. So, whatever practices you have that help you notice and stay in the present are useful tools in recovery. Perhaps it is spending time in nature or in an activity that helps you focus on your body or your breathing. Perhaps it is a hobby or a vocation. Build on these to include something daily that helps you focus on the present moment. This practice or activity of being present is like irrigation for the soul. A critical aspect of our spiritual recovery is that we nourish our inner life, our core, which is linked to the eternal now. Many spiritual teachers and writers concur on the "power of now", or the ever present now, and that everything else is an illusion. We will explore the important topics of states of consciousness and the practice of presence in chapters 3 and 4.

The following exercises relate to paying attention to our present experience, or being present to ourselves, and to being responsive to others, or responsible, able to respond. These are critical abilities that may be greatly underdeveloped, in light of the intense and deeply rooted conditioning to act according to what we believe will put on the best face for others.

ACT 2.12: CHARM SCHOOL

RASA survivors can be charming. Seriously. Before repressed memories flooded our consciousness (along with flashbacks, anxiety attacks, etc.) or public disclosures, I have no doubt that was the case for many survivors. However, during the anguish and frustration-filled process of learning more and more about our own experiences and others' neglect or collusion with our abuse, we may have lost that gentle sweetness that comes from our best self.

The following list may not apply to you, and I include it because it has served me as a concrete reminder of how to get along with others at times when my mind and life were so scrambled I was happy if I looked down at my feet and saw two matching shoes on them. That's a joke, and it's true. If you have managed to maintain the following and other positive interpersonal acts throughout the throes of your recovery, congratulate yourself. Otherwise, consider practicing the following behaviors with people whom you pass on the streets, share an elevator, bus or train ride with, or meet.

- Smile without expectation of a return smile;
- Say "hello" without expectation of a pleasant response;
- Say "excuse me" if you bump;
- Say "thank you" or "bless you" as appropriate;
- When driving, be courteous;
- Allow yourself to be generous with small acts of kindness, and then let them go with no expectation of external reward;
- Allow yourself to be playful in some small, simple, and natural way, and then let it go and take only the memory with you.

Sometimes, living in survival mode can keep us closed or self-centered. In various recovery programs, service to others is a key component. I think it builds on the previous acts of kindness and exercises in a more altruistic and more public way. Consider the following partial list of simple acts of service or "getting along with others" and practice whatever represents a new behavior for you. Afterwards, consider how it is congruent or incongruent with the best person you want to be.

- Pick up after yourself, or clean up a mess you've made;
- If someone else is cleaning up the mess they've made, help them out;
- Practice listening to others, especially when you feel the impulse to respond, and most especially when you feel the need to be right;
- Share something you like;
- When driving and the lanes merge, yield;
- Think of solutions that will help both others and you get something you will both want;
- When working or playing with others, celebrate someone else's achievement or special recognition;
- If you're having an especially tough time, communicate your recovery process with someone you trust, such as a therapist, family member, fellow survivor, etc.

SURVIVORS

SECTION TWO
HOW DO SURVIVORS VICTIMIZE OR RE-VICTIMIZE OURSELVES?

For me, one impact of religious authority sexual abuse has been that even though I functioned with relative educational and professional success, I lived a life akin to a religious prisoner who served a life sentence for something that was not my fault. For years after the abuse, I worked hard to be a good, if not the perfect, Catholic, as if my good behavior could release me from my toxic shame and prison sentence. However, I did not recognize or change self-damaging behavior that was linked to my damaged boundaries and reactions to abusive authority figures. I attempted to live in the present, to be a good person and be freed from my toxic shame, but worked with profound misperceptions of myself as a survivor, as helpless, hopeless, voiceless, powerless. It was difficult to acknowledge that I seemed to be attracted to or to create other opportunities to be abused, whether emotional, professional, etc. In short, I functioned as an adult child.

THINK: BEHAVIOR INVENTORY

Consider the following questions:

- Do I tend to commit too quickly?
- Alternatively, do I have a tendency to procrastinate and postpone, or drag out decisions?
- Am I inclined toward childlike or compulsive conformity, or to subservience?
- Do I tend toward adolescent rebelliousness or a desire to be different?
- Do depressive moods make me see everything in a bleak light, paralyzing me from acting?
- Do I tend toward an exaggerated sense of self-worth and to dreams of being a hero?
- On the contrary, do I have feelings of inferiority?
- Do I have a tendency to cut myself off from other people?
- Alternatively, do I take refuge in being overly social?
- Do I gravitate toward dependencies of any kind?
- Do I tend to be hyperactive?
- On the contrary, do I have a tendency to lack motivation or to run from situations and responsibility?
- Do I tend to have an excessive need for being admired?
- Do I have a tendency to suppress reality in order to flee into beautiful, perhaps pious dreams?
- On the contrary, do I tend to stare pessimistically, perhaps cynically, at the evils of the world so that I can no longer believe in any ideals?
- Do I have a tendency to exaggerate fears, or on the other hand, to be naïve or a daredevil?
- Am I given to spiritual fervor or to skeptical behavior that borders on a lack of faith?

ACT 2.20: SELF ASSESSMENT

Write what comes to mind for you related to up to five of the symptoms you have seen in your own life. What do you have to gain by changing these behaviors? What do you have to lose by changing these behaviors?

1. Gain_____

   Lose_____

2. Gain_____

   Lose_____

3. Gain_____

   Lose_____

4. Gain_____

   Lose_____

5. Gain_____

   Lose_____

THINK: ROLES WE PLAY

One of the characteristics of survivors of RASA is self-victimization. In a sense, we are prone to promote our own victimization because our boundaries have been or are extremely damaged, leaving us with an overdeveloped sense of protecting others or a non-existent sense of protecting ourselves. One picture of a person with damaged boundaries is a person who may be "all over the place", interpersonally or professionally. On the other hand, a picture of a person with damaged boundaries is the person who is "nowhere". In such circumstance, it is common for survivors to take on roles or patterns of behaviors that serve others, but are not in our best interest.

Carolyn Myss, in *Sacred Contracts*, identifies four archetypes that every person experiences. I will use these synonymously with roles. The four basic archetypes, or roles, are: **child, victim, saboteur,** and **prostitute.** I find these four roles helpful as ways to see stages of recovery from religious authority sexual abuse. Everyone literally experiences being a child, and to some degree, continues to act as a child — emotionally, intellectually, socially, and perhaps even sexually. If you are reading this book, I imagine that you also have the experience of victim. However, I do not imagine that the other two archetypes resonate readily with everyone's experiences; we will use all the archetypes in more metaphoric terms than literal.

Consider the immediate experiences of abuse, as discussed in chapter 1. Victims of child sexual abuse are voiceless and defenseless (child). We were emotionally and sexually taken advantage of by someone more powerful (victim). Knowingly or unknowingly, a victim of RASA disconnects from herself and her experience, making it impossible to report the crime (saboteur). Finally, we were used as a sexual object (prostitute). In each stage of recovery, it is possible to see how these archetypes operate differently and in ways that help us.

As adults, survivors often live with chronic feelings of low self-esteem and inadequacy, dependent upon others for their needs, and thereby vulnerable to others' whims. We seek others' decisions for us or make rash decisions without consideration to various perspectives (child). We act as if we are helpless. As adults, survivors are often cannon fodder in interpersonal, social or institutional conflicts. We live life as if that meant moving from crisis to crisis. We give notice at work, move out of the house with or without the children, and move in with relatives or into some other place. We act in ways that don't solve problems, but that instead postpone decisions (victim). We act as if we are hopeless.

As adults, survivors may act on compulsive attention-seeking behaviors and suicidal ideation, or act as martyrs or disposable pawns for a cause; survivors engage with others as intellectual, emotional or psychological killers (saboteur). We act as if we were purposeless. Likewise, many survivors turn to methods of numbing, such as substance abuse, promiscuity, runaway behaviors, allowing others to use them and see themselves as objects (prostitute) to get something, physical or emotional. We act as if we were meaningless.

Survivors may suffer as if we were helplessness, hopelessness, purposelessness and meaninglessness, and believe that it is someone else's fault. Meanwhile, others may see survivors as creating their own suffering. Our health is our own. In order to stop our suffering, we must take responsibility for managing our own boundaries.

For example, say I have the idea that I want to be healthy, but my diet and activity don't match my body type or my stated personal goals. If I accept the idea that I need to lose a few pounds, my solution might be to find a product to buy or take that doesn't require a real change in behavior (victim). I might subscribe to a diet and follow it mechanically in order to avoid an imminent health crisis or a perceived negative outcome (survivor).

Using Carolyn Myss' discussion of four basic archetypes, I will link some of my own experiences to the action logic of "survivorhood". I can see how I have acted as if I were dependent on others for information, opportunities, and experiences that I have allegedly wanted for myself (child). I can see how I have allowed myself to be invisible, and therefore be overlooked, or a silent casualty in various professional ventures (victim). At the same time, I have fallen into the trap of using my subsequent resentment to derail or oppose others' ideas because they weren't mine or didn't include me (saboteur). At the same time, I have allowed others to use my time, talent, and resources because I wanted to be liked or because I maintained a misplaced loyalty or overdeveloped sense of responsibility for them (prostitute).

I also identify with other archetypes: teacher, healer, artist and wizard. While these may sound more dignified than the other four archetypes, they may also be disastrous or limited by living at a level of survivorhood. For instance, the Latin root for teaching is *educare*, which means "to draw forth". Teaching from a level of survival resulted in argument, rather than discourse. At a level of surviving, helping or healing others has come at my expense, if my wounds didn't interfere with my capacity to see and understand what others needed. At survival level, I was less of an artist than an artisan who created trinkets out of raw material, my own experiences. Finally, a wizard in a survival state may be more like an orphaned, albeit gifted, child. I can appreciate that I saw myself as more developed in these areas than others saw or experienced. Living at a physical and emotional survival level can be a fragmented existence, and the full measure of our best selves comes through integration and transformation.

ACT 2.21: ARCHETYPES

What do you think your mission in life is supposed to be?

How do you see the basic archetypes or roles (Child, Victim, Prostitute, and Saboteur) enacted in your life?

See Carolyn Myss' descriptions of archetypes and find four archetypes or roles that you identify with to some degree. What is a strength of this archetype? What is a weakness or limitation?

THINK: RE-VICTIMIZATION

I hope it is fairly clear that survivors may victimize themselves in general. However, when survivors take up actions as a response to the abuse of authority, they often experience a re-victimization of the original sexual abuse by a religious authority. Earlier in this chapter, I referred to Dr. Woodson's comments, "When you control a man's thinking, you do not have to worry about his actions." The betrayal and abuse by a religious authority imprints a victim's thinking at such a profound level that subsequent approaches or interactions with authority figures and their supporters are loaded up with a primordial fight or flight response. As Dr. Woodson noted, our "education makes it necessary."

ACT 2.22: ABCS OF RE-VICTIMIZATION

There are many ways that RASA survivors can re-victimize themselves. The following is only a partial list. Read the list and underline any behaviors that relate to you.

Argue with others and with authorities who question your motives, experience, or pain;
Believe reports from the abuser's organization or public relations group; become a poster child for child sexual abuse; begin random conversations with people about the abuser;
Confront the abuser or superiors before being psychologically ready for such a direct action;
Deliver a public presentation about the abuse to strangers; deny that we are traumatized and may be vulnerable to the rejection or challenges that others may levy against us;
Expect quick results or resolution from any individual action;
Forget the abuser is very unhealthy and expect him or her to show compassion or understanding;
Go public without having given yourself time to develop a perspective of recovery and healing
Help everyone else in exposing the abuse without taking care of ourselves;
Identify only as a victim; you are not the abuse;
Jump into competitions over "whose pain is worse", a.k.a., the "Pain Olympics";
Kill off others, emotionally, socially, or professionally, instead of reviving or healing yourself;
Let others who don't care know about your past or present experiences around abuse;

Make abuse the first or only thing you talk about with others;

Never talk about abuse with others;

Overwhelm others with information about what has taken you and others years to understand;

Participate in dangerous or destructive "activism";

Quit therapy; question, "Why me?" In reality, the question is "why not me?";

Reply to all questions about your abuse with the same level of candor, trust and honesty;

Sacrifice your voice, feelings, and integrity so that others will like you;

Take the resistance or negative treatment of you, as you speak up for yourself, personally;

Underestimate the resistance to your and others' stories of abuse;

View others as the enemy, regardless of their behavior; violate your own boundaries;

Wish you were someone else;

Xplain away abusive behavior;

Yell at people who remind you of the abuser;

Zero out your checking or savings account, or health or sleep or patience account, way before the end of the month.

THINK: RE-VICTIMIZATION IN RETROSPECT

When the flashbacks and other experiences listed at the beginning of this chapter become undeniable, victims begin to speak up. This was the point at which I began to admit to myself and those I cared for, and who cared for me, that I was suffering. That is when I began to speak out publicly, perhaps prematurely, to bring clergy sexual abuse to light. I say "perhaps prematurely" because, the more I spoke up about my abuse and "wrongful imprisonment", the more religious people effectively acted as the metaphoric prison guards. In this way, I re-victimized myself.

The documentary "After Innocence" chronicles how some people have been wrongly accused, imprisoned, and have served decades of life sentences before they were exonerated. This reminds me of my "survivor" experience, in that as much as I told my story, very few people seemed to believe or want to believe me. Many RASA victims live through or survive someone else's crime of sexual abuse. Survivors live in a psychological and social prison among people who fervently believe in the system and in the authorities of this system.

Survivors step away from "victimhood" when they come to believe in their own experience more than in others' perceptions. For many, identifying with the term "survivor", and not "vic-

tim", is an important step. The good news is that this is not the end of the road towards health and happiness. The bad news is also that this is not the end of the road towards health and happiness.

Re-victimization happens in two ways. The first way relates to external factors that I referred to in chapter 1. External events, people, places, or things, may trigger a wide range of uncontrollable emotion for a RASA survivor: sadness, anger, confusion, a sense of being overwhelmed, grief, etc. that a victim of sexual abuse may have buried or denied for so many years. However, with support, these feelings may be managed and redeemed in the sense that the feelings do not remain toxic and may be useful in the work of ending RASA.

Recovery from child sexual abuse involves a shift from denial to awareness, and from awareness to taking action to help ourselves, and from taking action to help ourselves to taking action to helping someone else and to end child abuse. Survivors take action in order to move beyond being victimized. It may be badly done, so to speak, but it's a step away from being voiceless, powerless, worthless, and hopeless, and towards voice, agency, self-worth, and hope. Sometimes such an action is met with support from others, and the step is liberating.

Even with support, the process of engaging with others about the sexual abuse may be painful and may trigger new painful memories. In this way, the healing process is counter-intuitive. Why would anyone "want" to talk with someone about their experiences and consequences of abuse, knowing that it may be painful and trigger new painful memories? My experience is that there is good news in this process because many survivors experience it as cathartic, albeit very difficult. Note well: cathartic, not magical.

On the other hand, when such action is met with skepticism, hostility, minimization, denial, defensiveness, disbelief, etc., the action is hurtful and frustrating, perhaps infuriating and maddening. This can trigger feelings of re-victimization. Some survivors continue to put themselves in positions of being "on the front lines", as if we do not know that others may not be supportive of our witness. In fact, others may tell us what is good for us, tell us what we want, blame us for our experiences, blame us for victimizing them or the church, temple, etc. This behavior relates

to the second day of the sidewalk story in that survivors can pretend that we don't see the hole in the sidewalk that we know is there. This is the self- or re-victimizing behavior of an adult child.

At this point I can say with certainty that the job or responsibility of a survivor of religious authority sexual abuse is to stop victimizing or re-victimizing her or himself. I can now see how the admonition, "Stop hitting yourself! Stop hitting yourself! Why are you still hitting yourself?" related to me when I consider my own drive to rescue others. When I began to feel the full weight of my rage breaking into my consciousness and emotional life thirty years after the sexual abuse, I did everything I could to unmask and to speak to the past abuse and current cover up or denial that put more children at risk. I can now see that a barometer of my need to be healed was my zeal in reaching out to others and taking care of others and doing my best to help others who were also abused, without taking care of myself.

ACT 2.23: NOTICE WHEN YOU ARE OVERLOADED

Pay attention to your experiences. Notice when you are overloaded, when you miss information or forget something that someone said, etc. Being overloaded with thoughts or feelings is normal, or something that everyone experiences at various times. For survivors, this may be disabling. When this happens, look around and find a place where you can step aside from the activity or stimulus. Breathe slowly and deeply, breathing in love, and breathing out peace. Find those spaces regularly wherever you go and use them, even if it is only for a moment.

SECTION THREE
WHAT ARE SOME IMPLICATIONS OF
SELF VICTIMIZATION AND RE-VICTIMIZATION?

THINK: SCREAMING FIRE

Consider the analogy of screaming, "Fire! Fire!" in a building. When I began to speak to people about the abuse that had happened in their place of worship, I thought I was warning people to notice that they were in a burning building. In my mind the firefighters, or religious authorities, who were supposed to be bringing people out of a burning building were either taking a cigarette break and joking around, or comforting one another about the damage done to their place of worship.

There was a movie many years ago about a firefighter who was an arsonist, called "Back-draft." It raised the unspeakable danger that one of the people designated to protect and serve was actually starting a fire or impeding the work of putting it out. Isn't that the unspeakable? This scenario, at this time of my recovery, was interchangeable with religious authorities and those who unknowingly or knowingly perpetuate religious authority child sexual abuse. I felt the need to rescue people, to announce that there was a crisis in my church.

In my mind, there was a current and present danger. For many churchgoers, the fire had burned out a long time ago. I can now see a dual consciousness about the same recognized issue —religious authority sexual abuse. As a survivor, I could only see the corruption in the very institutions that many people believed were pure, beyond reproach, and deserving of all our

support for the good of society.

We want to believe that accountants and auditors don't "cook the books". We want to believe that teachers don't cheat and "cook the test scores" or abuse children. We want to believe that business leaders have the common good as a shared value. We want believe that our government leaders do not lie, and we entrust them with great power. We do not want to believe that religious leaders would sexually violate children and betray their congregations.

So when I, as a survivor, raised the alarm, my experience was that no one wanted to believe there was corruption in this one house, because that would mean that there may be corruption in the other houses as well. And so when I spoke louder or tried harder to make inroads with many churchgoers, it seemed that I was running into a brick wall, an invisible wall, but a wall of thick resistance. That silly book title, *Stop hitting yourself! Stop hitting yourself! Why are you still hitting yourself?* described my re-victimizing actions. I was projecting my pain or woundedness onto other survivors and saving them, because I desperately needed to be saved and extinguish the fires in my own ravaged soul. My wounds from a long time ago, my lost spiritual limbs, were still fresh in my mind and my psyche. I needed to take care of myself, but instead I was doing everything possible to take care of others.

ACT 2.30: GIVING AND RECEIVING

In the following section, I identify some common impacts on boundaries, approaches to authority figures and the roles that survivors of religious authority sexual abuse take up, even after the abuse has physically ended. To do so, I have taken a few habits that self-actualization gurus have identified as related to health and happiness and I have linked them to prior discussions, as seen by comparing possible victim and survivor behaviors. I will refer to these in future chapters as manifestations of recovery.

1. Give people more than they expect and do it cheerfully (Purpose or Agency).	
Victims: Stealing from others.	Survivors: Hording, giving to get.

What comes to mind for you related to any of the symptoms you have seen in your own life?

How have you been mis-educated in your learning of these behaviors?

What do you have to gain by changing these behaviors? What do you have to lose by changing these behaviors?

2. Don't believe all you hear, spend all you have or sleep all you want (Purpose or self-worth).	
Victims: Live addictive lifestyle; live self or other destructive lifestyle.	Survivors: Live an excessive lifestyle; live a consumeristic lifestyle (buying what others are selling).

What comes to mind for you related to any of the symptoms you have seen in your own life?

How have you been mis-educated in your learning of these behaviors?

What do you have to gain by changing these behaviors? What do you have to lose by changing these behaviors?

3. Never laugh at anyone's dream. People who don't have dreams don't have much (Self-worth or voice).

Victims: Steal, crush, or compete with others' dreams.	Survivors: Follow others' dreams, rather than believing and sharing our dreams with others.

What comes to mind for you related to any of the symptoms you have seen in your own life?

How have you been mis-educated in your learning of these behaviors?

What do you have to gain by changing these behaviors? What do you have to lose by changing these behaviors?

---

4.   Love deeply and passionately. You might get hurt but it's the only way to live life completely (Purpose).

Victims: Abuse our own or others' minds, hearts, and bodies.	Survivors: Live to not get hurt or to not lose, control, rather than loving ourselves mind, heart, and body.

What comes to mind for you related to any of the symptoms you have seen in your own life?

How have you been mis-educated in your learning of these behaviors?

What do you have to gain by changing these behaviors? What do you have to lose by changing these behaviors?

5. When someone asks you a question you don't want to answer, smile and ask, "Why do you want to know?" (Purpose or Voice)	
Victims: Debate or argue to win.	Survivors: Discuss or debate to learn or get more of something, rather than dialogue to understand, learn or join with.

What comes to mind for you related to any of the symptoms you have seen in your own life?

How have you been mis-educated in your learning of these behaviors?

What do you have to gain by changing these behaviors? What do you have to lose by changing these behaviors?

6. Remember that great love and great achievements involve great risk (Purpose or self-worth).	
Victims: Live to please or not make mistakes.	Survivors: Live to "get it right," be good or recognized, rather than living to learn and learning to live.

What comes to mind for you related to any of the symptoms you have seen in your own life?

How have you been mis-educated in your learning of these behaviors?

What do you have to gain by changing these behaviors? What do you have to lose by changing these behaviors?

SURVIVORS

7. Remember the three R's: Respect for self; Respect for others; and responsibility for all your actions (Purpose or agency).	
Victims: Live from crisis to crisis.	Survivors: Live to navigate or beat the system.
What comes to mind for you related to any of the symptoms you have seen in your own life?	
How have you been mis-educated in your learning of these behaviors?	
What do you have to gain by changing these behaviors? What do you have to lose by changing these behaviors?	

Thoughts to live by (of your choice)	
Victims:	Survivors:
What comes to mind for you related to this symptom in your own life?	
How have you been mis-educated in your learning of these behaviors?	
What do you have to gain by changing these behaviors? What do you have to lose by changing these behaviors?	

Malcolm Gladwell, in his book *Blink*, offers many examples of how smart people make instantaneous interpretations of the world around them that are absolutely wrong. Some of these interpretations are based on a bias that whatever we don't readily understand, we ascribe as something else easily describable: as dumb, as ugly, as wrong, etc. In addition, some interpretations or behaviors are short-circuited because a person is in a state of high stress. This is part of the reason that most law enforcement officers do not engage in high speed chases; in that elevated stress state, well-thought out safety practices are lost and people get hurt.

Survivors suffer from a profound imprint or distortion in our ways of understanding and making sense of experience. Survivors' lived experiences are often impacted by triggers of past high-stress trauma of abuse by religious authority. A profound shame-based imprint on our sense of self distorts our ways of working with others through issues of: control, perfection, blaming others, denial, unreliability, incompleteness, no talking, etc.

When I examine myself and my "who am I?" answers, and I say "parent", I must look closely at what that means for other people, how other people have experienced me or my parenting. While I can and must have compassion for myself and other survivors of religious authority sexual abuse who share behaviors related to shame, I must also take responsibility for my present day activities. First, I must examine how the lack of control I had growing up has influenced or influences ways that I seek control as an adult, and as a parent. As a result of religious authority sexual abuse, I felt profoundly ashamed of myself, and so I need to ask how I have tried to be perfect in some ways,

and how that has infected my way of parenting. Because I strove to be perfect, an unrealistic and unhealthy aspiration, I developed a habit of blaming others for problems or my own unhappiness. I had no real skills to deal with the profound unhappiness and rage that fester within me, and so I found fault with others. As a parent, I gave out more blame than was ever deserved.

Because I was in denial of my own experience, I was in denial about any feedback that did not fit into my self-image as a parent or the images I had of my children. Because my family boundaries and my personal boundaries were so poor and damaged, I have been unreliable in many ways as a parent, shifting my boundaries from lax to strict without even recognizing it. Another expression of profound shame is the incompleteness of behaviors or efforts. This, for me, has shown in not following up with various basic parental responsibilities, having poor supervision or absence. As I grew up not able to talk about my family of origin dysfunction, and, of course, not able to talk about the abuse or any other inappropriate interaction with the religious authority who molested me, I learned to not talk about many things as a spouse or parent.

I can now see how deeply imprinted my shame-based behaviors have been. The following activity is intended to strengthen and nurture those areas in you that have been impacted by shame. Think about the ways that you have brought control to others, or ways that others have experienced you as controlling. Now call upon love and compassion for yourself. Let love for yourself be like the pure oxygen that you need to breathe in, in order to breathe out that love, vs. control, in your actions with others.

SURVIVORS

- Think of ways that you have held or promoted unrealistic expectations for yourself and for others of being perfect. Now breathe in the pure oxygen of acceptance of your imperfection so that you can breathe that acceptance to others in their imperfection.

- Think of the ways that you have been blaming others. Breathe in the pure oxygen of support for yourself so that you can be supportive of others when things don't go the way you had hoped.

- Think of the ways that you have acted in denial of the pain that you have brought to others and yourself. Breathe in the pure oxygen of vulnerability that makes you human, so you can be careful with others or ability.

- Because our boundaries have been so damaged and are unreliable, think of how you can be more reliable to do what you say you will do. Think of ways that you can be clearer about your boundaries about who you are and what is appropriate for you to do. Take advantage of the opportunities to work with boundaries that are already clear, so that you will be more and more able to set and manage your own boundaries.

- Consider the ways that your communication or actions have been incomplete; think of ways that you can learn from others good communication or good follow through. Let yourself learn and strengthen this part of your identity in simple ways. Consider the ways that you have not talked in the past, as if it were a kind of breathing. To not talk would be like inhaling only and not exhaling. To overcompensate and say everything that is on our minds would be like exhaling continuously.

REFLECT: I STILL LOVE YOU ANYWAY

Survivor behaviors remind me of Dr. Woodson's comments, "When you control a man's thinking, you do not have to worry about his actions … In fact, if there is no back door, he will cut one for his special benefit. His education makes it necessary." In the following section, I offer several thoughts and practices that can help you re-educate yourself with respect to being hopeful, purposeful, helpful, and meaningful.

Before moving to the next section, however, revisit the activity in chapter one, "I love you anyway". By now you may have identified several areas in your experiences that don't feel good or serve you well anymore. Consider that your current insight or understandings are part of a healing, learning, developing process. You are becoming the change you wish to see in the world. It is a process and you are moving through it.

SECTION FOUR
WHAT CAN YOU DO?

Developmentally, RASA victims often bury knowledge of sexual abuse and an understanding of its impacts far from consciousness. When becoming conscious of the abuse, or when making it public knowledge, survivors can see or use these toxic experiences as if they were their major life story. This challenges what religious authority supporters believe as the dominant religious story and leaves survivors acting as if our past victimization were only our story.

THINK: ABCs TOWARDS HEALTH

To the degree that you identify with your past victimization as your story, as who you are, I encourage you to consider that your health and happiness may be a casualty or cost of such an identity. Let me be clear: Naming what has happened to you is important, but holding onto the toxicity of these painful memories as your story is unhealthy. Practice and think about the following list of exercises that may help you identify a new role or archetype that gives you new life or energy. Then write what you want regarding your safety, health, and happiness. This is a way to name and live a new chapter in your life story.

Allow yourself time to mourn, feel and understand what happened to you; ask for help;

Become a friend to yourself;

Consider being safe, healthy, and happy;

Do something in a natural setting that helps soothe your soul;

Expand your vocabulary to include words of affirmation for yourself and others;

Fix something in your environment that needs attention;

Get help with an area of self-improvement;

Hope, dream, laugh, live;

Imagine being safe, healthy, and happy;

Join a group that affirms a healthy behavior that you want more of in your life;

Keep a daily practice of self care (physical, mental, emotional, spiritual);

Let go of the there and then, there and now, and here and then;

Make a plan to be;

Notice when you are on overload and take care of yourself

Own your part in your misery and happiness;

Plan being safe, healthy, and happy; practice self care;

Quit doing for other people what they can do for themselves;

Reach out to others in ways that are safe; relax;

Set up personal boundaries before engaging in activities;

Take time to consider that others might be in therapy because of you;

Use the resources that are available to you to be safe and healthy;

Visualize being a resource for others, having enough love, hope, and wisdom to share;

Work every day on using your time, talents, and resources for healing;

Xtend compassion to people whom you may not like;

Yield to "being happy", if "being right and unhappy" is the other choice;

Zero out your account of resentments by the end of each day.

Use the grids to identify and plan new behaviors.

ABC behavior to live by (of your choice)
Who or what is a good example of this behavior?
What is something I can do to practice or apply this behavior in the near future?
What do you have to gain by changing these behaviors? What do you have to lose by changing these behaviors?

ABC behavior to live by (of your choice)
Who or what is a good example of this behavior?
What is something I can do to practice or apply this behavior in the near future?
What do you have to gain by changing these behaviors? What do you have to lose by changing these behaviors?

ABC behavior to live by (of your choice)
Who or what is a good example of this behavior?
What is something I can do to practice or apply this behavior in the near future?
What do you have to gain by changing these behaviors? What do you have to lose by changing these behaviors?

In chapter 1, I asked you to consider the past abuse and to work with the experience in order to recognize what is likely linked to present day flashbacks, anxiety attacks, moments of disorientation, etc. In the following activity, focus on the one person who manages to push your buttons and thus get you worked up, emotionally speaking. Use this person to gain more insight about yourself and explore the self-change you need to engage in to help you connect more effectively by responding, where you choose an appropriate behavioral response, rather than reacting, where your emotions dictate your behavioral response, to that person's inappropriate behavior. The following example may help you begin your own self-assessment and transformation of your present day experiences.

1   **Situational Context** (Who, what, when, where, why)
    In a brief paragraph, describe or outline the circumstances involving you, the person, and any other players.

    Incident: This Thanksgiving weekend I had plans of having a dinner on Sunday for my children and then going back to cook Thanksgiving dinner for my mother and family. My boyfriend, who is 40 years old and has never been married nor has any children, does not get along with all my children. This was a family get together I was having, which included him, but he does not like my son, Bill.

2   **Triggers** (external and internal); the trigger can be both external and internal. The internal trigger refers to your emotional state prior to the situational context. For example, if you left home in an uptight mood because of a fight with your partner, parent, sibling, or child, your thoughts and emotions may be focused on this experience; therefore, you may be in a sour mood when you walk into the context in question. Emotional states can therefore be either positive or negative depending on the

quality of your relationships or the quality of your other environments, wuch as at work.

External triggers refer to the other person's behaviors that pushed your buttons. What did he or she say that got you worked up? What negative behaviors did he or she engage in?

Trigger: I was preparing dinner when my boyfriend suddenly came and told me, "If your son, Bill, shows up I am going to leave."

3   **Physiological Response**
    Under stress, the body produces cortisol and adrenaline, chemicals that can contribute to a fight-flight-freeze response. As the brain stem controls reflexive responses, your body may respond with an accelerated heart beat, higher blood pressure, tense muscles, changed breathing pattern, sweating, etc. Monitor your bodily response.

    Bodily reaction: I instantly started to have an anxiety attack. I felt like I was out of breath.

4   **Self-Talk**
    What do you say to yourself every time this person acts up? It's okay, in this assignment, to confess that you actually entertained a few choice swear words to describe how you were feeling in that particular point in time. It's very important that you bring to consciousness the self-talk you typically engage in, more so under stress.

    Self-talk: I was able to gain my composure and react by thinking and self-talk. I said to myself, Jim, you dirty bastard, why are you trying to wreck this day? Get the fuck out right now. I said to myself, "Calm down, calm down."

SURVIVORS

5 Emotions

Which feelings come to the fore? Anger? Anger is usually a secondary response as underlying anger is a mixture of other feelings that are already being contaminated by your internal trigger or mood prior to this encounter. Underlying anger is from such feelings as annoyance, irritation, hurt, grief, etc.

Emotions: I was angry and hurt because I thought this situation with my children and him was getting better. However, I did not let my emotions take control of me.

6 Behavioral Response

What was your first behavioral response to this person's negative behavior? Did you ignore him or her because you weren't too sure how to handle him or her? Did you order him or her to leave your presence?

My behavior: I turned and looked at him and gently said, "Jim, you are free to go anytime if you want. I have no control over you; you make your own decisions and please, if you don't want to be with my children, remember nobody is forcing you into it. I have a relationship with you and my children."

7 The effect of your behavior on the other

How did your response affect the other person? How did he or she, in turn, respond to you? How did your response change over a period of time?

His behavior: He said he could not believe the way I reacted to his proposal of leaving. He said he wanted to make it clear that he did not want to feel pressured into staying and he apologized and said he would stay. I told him, "whatever", but if he feels uneasy just leave anyway.

He told me he sees a change in me in a way that I am not over-emotional anymore. He told me he loves me and that if I need my space, all I have to do is say it. We then had a talk and made an agreement that I only see him twice a month.

I finished cooking dinner and my children started arriving. I was feeling a little anxious wondering if Bill, my son, was going to show up.

Effect on Family: The doorbell rang and anxiety started to set in; sure enough, it was Bill. He walked in and gave his two sisters and brother a hug. He grabbed me and gave me an enormous hug and looked around and asked where Jim was. Jim came out from the washroom and Bill walked up to him and gave him a big hug, too. I stood back and observed, and, having eye contact with Jim, I knew he was going to be okay. My children kept him occupied while I set the table.

I felt comfortable while we ate and sat around, knowing full well that my children were trying hard to accept Jim as my boyfriend. After my children had left, my boyfriend said, "I saw you observing and I'll tell you the truth, I am starting to like your children." My dinner turned out well.

8 Family of Origin Insight

a) What does this person's behavior and your response remind you of when you were that person's age (if he or she is younger), especially as it pertains to the way your parents or other authority figures responded to you or your siblings? Are there any similarities between your response and your parenting style or your parents' parenting style?

b) What is the connection between that person's negative behavior and that person's family environment?

Family of Origin Insight: The next day, I went and had a talk with my mother after I had cooked dinner. I asked her why my dad's other children, older than we, did not come around too often. She said because she did not like them. I just sat there listening to her talk about them and I understood where the jealousy of my children was passed on from. My mother had my dad sandwiched between us and his other children from his first wife.

9 Self-Reflection

What insight about yourself did this person pass on to you? How did you change?

Self-Reflection: I am learning a lot about myself as a person. I am doing a lot of self-work. I would normally be very emotional and very defensive for my children in this Thanksgiving situation or any other time.

I would have felt uneasy, filled with anxiety that would have ruined my day if I had not done any self-work. I truly believe now, going back and talking to my mother and family, mainly observing, I can understand why I am undifferentiated. I can see how my dad was sandwiched by my family just the way my children and boyfriend tried doing to me. I am going up on the scale of differentiation and I love it. I can think for myself, take control of my emotions and boundaries.

ACT 2.41: TRIGGERS

Use the guide (steps 1-9) to study some of your own reactions and new behaviors.

Situational Context (Who, what, when, where, why)

Triggers (external and internal); the trigger can be both external and internal.

Physiological Response

Self-Talk

Emotions

Behavioral Response

The effect of your behavior on the other(s)

Family of Origin Insight

Self Reflection

SURVIVORS

In this chapter, I have given you a preliminary context of a learning and development process. Victims are often blind to their own abuse, or we don't know what we don't know, while survivors struggle with the hidden understanding related to their abuse, or we don't know what we know. With respect to self-understanding, victims suffer from a kind of illiteracy, while survivors who have learned to get along for so long are beginning to see the limits to the identities that others have given them. This chapter's aim was to increase your appreciation of the ways you have internalized abuse, and then to imagine a new vision of yourself.

While dealing and reeling with the painful process of active recovery from child sexual abuse, many survivors remain isolated or meet denial or rejection from those who have informal or formal authority to address the abuse. The feelings of being spiritually or emotionally imprisoned are unpleasant and useful. In this journey, this spiritual journey, we may find ourselves in what some call a "desert experience", seeking but not finding inner peace. The peace or comfort that you may long for may feel lost or stolen from you. All these experiences are part of this recovery process, as they may push us to seek help. As Martin Luther King, Jr. once said, "Freedom is never voluntarily given by the oppressor; it must be demanded by the oppressed." We must demand our freedom from ourselves.

Even in the face of flashbacks, anxiety attacks, or other obvious experiences of being disabled or feeling incompetent, it may be difficult to ask for help. Welcome to the club. Get help anyway. While you may have been helpless at some point, and that may have been directly related to your abuse, you are not helpless now. By getting help, you will be able to give help appropriately in the future.

You are not Helpless
You are not Voiceless
You are not Purposeless
You are not Worthless

If you have not already found a support group or begun to work with a professional therapist, I encourage you to do so. Undigested emotions, like undigested food, are toxic. Take time for yourself to breathe; take time to think before you act. You've been working in survival mode for too long; it is time to rejuvenate. Take time to be quiet, to pay attention to self, heart, feelings, etc. In daily interactions with others, pay attention to when you have a strong reaction to someone or something.

Congratulations on your journey to this point. You are beautiful, brilliant, talented, free to be curious, a spiritual being having a human experience, a gentle soul, a gift from God, a spark of God, pure consciousness, a manifestation of spirit in the process of healing your humanity. There is a time to mourn the past and it may be that you mourn your present. There is a time to hope, to dream, to laugh, and to live. The next chapter will focus on making the choice to live.

Share your thoughts on this book & possibly win prizes.
Everyone who shares ideas on how to make this workbook better
will get a free copy of the next edition of the book.
Go to www.HTSAH.com or www.HealingTheSexuallyAbusedHeart.com

CHAPTER THREE
SURVIVOR-THRIVERS

INTRODUCTION

I ended chapter 1 with a health analogy in which victims are in a position of needing immediate support, perhaps a blood transfusion. As adult victims, we can look back and mourn the loss or death of that childhood and foundational innocence. I ended chapter 2 with the admonition that survivors might think about helping others, but begin by helping themselves. Working through a survivor experience involves recognizing and mourning our present victimization, self-victimization, unproductive conflicts, rage, and all the things that we hold onto that do not serve us.

This chapter raises the questions, "What do you want and what do you choose?" By recognizing that our own desire is a seed or spark of the Spirit, we have a choice either to honor and work with our desire, or to fight against or flee from what we want. We have a choice about seeking others' counsel, which is part of living more intentionally. Given what I want, how do I utilize wisdom, beyond the wisdom I have been applying up to this point? What wisdom from elders, or others with more experience and insight, meditation, contemplation, or other sources is available to me?

Do you want to live well and do no harm? Do you want to live in harmony with all around you, not taking offense when no offense was intended? Will you only fight when it is right to do so, and in the right way? Then you must choose to live intentionally, tapping into a deeper spirituality that links you to the universe of wisdom that is inside you and around you. This is profound spiritual work, accessed through or beyond your past and present suffering.

This chapter deals with recognizing your part in feeding the behavior patterns that are not helpful to you. Survivor-thrivers work through deep wounds to live healthier lives of recovery. Survivor-thrivers may fall back into the hole in the sidewalk of old wounds and old experiences. But Survivors live as Survivor-thrivers by letting go of the toxic and shameful baggage associated with being abused that we have carried. This is a pivotal stage, a time for us to transform our own survival thinking and behaving as our own enemy into what some call living at a level of choice, responsibility or intentionality.

There is an expression that "the reason people blame things on previous generations is that there's only one other choice." We are responsible for our lives, our happiness. Being responsible means living with the ability to respond, the ability to adjust, the ability to adapt. It means that we have at least a basic understanding of the context in which we live, and that we have thought about how we would like to move forward. For RASA survivor-thrivers, it means that we will no longer be victims and we cannot deny our past abuse.

A goal of this chapter is to help you understand that your experiences, reactions, and what you know, this information, is actually in-formation. In fact we are in formation. This chapter assumes the basic awareness that victims have about the abuse and the hyper-sensitivity that survivors often have about living with the impacts of religious authority sexual abuse. It focuses on the integrative process that helps transform these open wounds towards scars or signs of abuse that are not toxic.

Your job as a Survivor-thriver is to integrate various parts of your best self into the same life. This integrative work leads to a healthy and balanced lifestyle. You are so worth it.

THINK: THE TWO WOLVES

An old grandfather said to his grandson, who came to him angry at a friend who had done him an injustice, "Let me tell you a story. I too, at times, have felt a great hate for those that have taken so much, with no sorrow for what they do. But hate wears you down, and does not hurt your enemy. It is like taking poison and wishing your enemy would die. I have struggled with these feelings many times."

He continued, "It is as if there are two wolves inside me. One is good and does no harm. He lives in harmony with all around him, and does not take offense when no offense was intended. He will only fight when it is right to do so, and in the right way. But the other wolf, ah! He is full of anger. The littlest thing will set him into a fit of temper. He fights everyone, all the time, for no reason. He cannot think because his anger and hate are so great. It is helpless anger, for his anger will change nothing. Sometimes, it is hard to live with these two wolves inside me, for both of them try to dominate my spirit."

The boy looked intently into his Grandfather's eyes and asked, "Which one wins, Grandfather?"

The Grandfather smiled and quietly said, "The one I feed."

ACT 3.00: WHAT DO I WANT?

Being a survivor-thriver is a relatively good problem to have. In addition to the question, "who am I?" survivor-thrivers are more able to answer the difficult question, what do I want? The idea in this exercise is for you to come up with as many answers as you can to the same question that are true for you, and not to come up with a "right" answer. The purpose of this exercise is to practice being intentional for ourselves. After coming up with your list of responses, I encourage you to share and assess those responses with a sponsor, therapist or another person whom you trust. Even if you don't have someone in mind at this point, do the exercise as it will spark a shift in your thinking about yourself and your well being now.

What do I want?

What do I want?

What do I want?

What do I want?

What do I want?

What do I want?

What do I want?

What do I want?

What do I want?

What do I want?

What do I want?

What do I want?

THINK: DESIRES

It may be difficult for RASA survivor-thrivers to answer the question, "What do I want?" It requires recognizing or tapping into our deep desires, those things which bring passion into our lives. Anything related to desire may trigger painful memories of our abuse, as our abusers' desire brought destruction into our lives. On the other hand, we may have ambivalence about enjoying our bodies or feelings, as they are linked to something shameful or sinful. It is important for us, as we are developing healthy boundaries, to also recognize and celebrate our desires.

Our soul is the source of our desire. God is the source of our soul. Victims or survivors may confuse many things with the objects of our desire, as is the case with any kind of addict, for example, people addicted to power, excitement, pleasure, etc. My emphasis on claiming our desire is like when a doctor searches for someone's pulse. Our desire is linked to our deep intentionality, which for now we can think of as what guides our best self.

A way to identify our desire or soul is to think of gifts that we know we have or that others tell us we have. Gifts are not just talents or things that you do well for show or for sale. Gifts are things that bring us and others true moments of enjoyment. Once we accept that we have desires or wants that are good and rooted in our best self, we can enjoy these. As we allow ourselves to enjoy our spirit, or soul, we can reconnect with enthusiasm and the ecstasy that addicts seek in search for God. We can begin to know the joy of

being out of our heads and into our bodies, and reintegrating our whole selves.

Eckhart Tolle, in *A New Earth: Awakening to Your Life's Purpose*, shares a perspective about attracting negative experiences, given our identification with a negative self-image. We have been impacted or infused with the negative energy of shame. There may be multiple layers of trauma or abuse that we're dealing with, so each layer that we release frees up more of our best self, as well as the challenges of moving beyond our fears, for example of false expectations appearing real.

Deepak Chopra, in *The Seven Spiritual Laws of Yoga*, encourages us to study our actions as they impact our own lives. He asks, "What are the consequences of the choice I'm making? Which choice is most likely to bring happiness and fulfillment to me and to those affected by my choice?" Then, he advises the reader to listen to "your heart for guidance and be guided by its message of comfort or discomfort. Your heart is the junction point between your mind and your body. If the choice feels comfortable in your body, move into it with confidence."

Do you desire to live well and do no harm? Do you desire to live in harmony with all around you, not taking offense when no offense was intended? Do you desire only to fight when it is right to do so, and in the right way? Do you desire to integrate various parts of your best self into the same life? When I was at my wits end related to where my recovery had brought me,

I needed to answer the basic questions "Who am I?", and "What do I want?" differently. What I came to realize was that I was like the Jimmy Stewart character in "It's a Wonderful Life", saying, "Please, God. I want to live." Do you want to live? Do you desire to live a healthy and balanced lifestyle? You are so worth it.

Religious authority sexual abuse has led us to the ground floor of authority issues, and as we tap into our souls, we open the door to move beyond religious authority into cosmic, divine and unity authority. We begin to let go of long-standing resentments or grievances. Forgiveness happens naturally when we see that grievances are burdensome to ourselves, feeding the cancer we have been given, feeding the wolf of suffering. When we focus on the present moment or on the presence in and around us, we are released from the illusion of past and future.

It is counter-intuitive that our loss has opened up our spirit, our true identity, our best self. But part of what it means to be a survivor-thriver is to see our past and find and create meaning on our own.

Part of what it means to be a survivor-thriver is to be rooted in our being, instead of lost in our mind, our past or our future. There, we know who we are not —victim, object of the universe— and who we are —spirit, subject of the universe. We get glimpses into the cosmic or Christ consciousness. We gain insight into the admonition that "to get what you really want, agree that what you have is what you want." We accept that the source of all abundance is not outside us, but it is in and around us. We can find joy in the raw fury of life and find sparks of God in the lava meeting the ocean in the timeless and brutal creation of new land. We begin to feel emotional weight loss, or a lightness of being. We can be inspired by space and the stars, as inklings of the space and stars in ourselves, if we so desire.

ACT 3.01: CHOICES I MAKE

In the story of the wolves, there might be only two choices. For example, "Do I participate in activities that are fragmenting or integrating? Do I try to become a person of success or become a person of value?" This activity is to help you consider how some of the following choices relate to you and how it might be possible to find another way, a third way, a way that begins to reconcile and integrate opposite views to find new possibilities.

How do I relate to others?	Dependent	Independent	Interdependent
Materially			
Emotionally			
Intellectually			
Spiritually			

How do I use what I have?	Hoard	Give away	Share
Materially			
Emotionally			
Intellectually			
Spiritually			

How do I work with problems?	Escape	Fight	Work with
Materially			
Emotionally			
Intellectually			
Spiritually			

SECTION ONE
WHAT IS LIVING AT A LEVEL OF CHOICE?

Survivor-thrivers become able to work effectively with our daily schedules or choices, neither denying our power or formal authority, nor resisting and fighting against power and formal authority as identified in others. The story of the wolves helps us think of living with responsibility with our internal wolves or reactions. Living responsively or at a level of choice also means examining our responses to external wolves or challenges, but not in a reactive way that victims or survivors experience.

THINK: LIVING BY CHOICE

The following example helps me understand living at a level of choice. Imagine planning a vacation to visit places you have heard about and researched, or to places you have been and want to return to because they are so life-giving and fill you with inspiration, joy, or pleasure. You plan accordingly for the designated amount of time you have, study how to get to those places, and choose where you'll stay. You are careful not to pack your schedule so that the activities would take away from those distinctive visits, whether they are with people or places or just time alone.

Taking the trip, there may be interruptions due to weather or other unforeseen changes, but you have the resources to figure out how to adjust your schedule, take care of yourself and get to the next place. When something comes up that means that your original plans cannot be met, you are able to understand your part in allowing that to happen and to learn from it. There is no real reason for whining or blaming. In truth, even conflicts are areas that open up new learning; they are areas that require attention, which can lead to more understanding of our own choices.

This is the beauty of planning and enjoying your trip. If something surprising happens along the way, it is all part of the trip that you have always wanted to have. Even if there are disturbing things that happen, they are not the trip. Those things are not everything. On this journey, there may be times of indescribable awe and joy and satisfaction, as well as adjustment or disappointment. You are your own travel agent, guide, and concierge.

ACT 3.10: PLANNING FOR TOMORROW

How does the idealistic scenario of planning a vacation relate to day to daily living, since vacation often doesn't relate to day to daily living? To make your choices clearer, think of tomorrow, for example, as a day that you have planned. It doesn't matter if the day holds meetings that you "have to" attend, or work that you "have to" show up for. Whatever the day holds, imagine that it is exactly what you have planned. As such, you have the material for the following exercise.
Given the things I have to do in the next 24 hours, what do I get out of ____?

What do I need to do to enjoy ____?

What is my backup or alternative plan if my participation in ____ becomes disempowering, energy draining or negative?

It is now up to you to beef up some areas before, during or after your activities. Think of alternatives for how you typically approach your activities, to the degree that you do not enjoy them. How you approach the next 24 hours and all it holds is your choice.

What can I do before _____ so that I can be ready and effective in that task?

During the task, how will I know that I am doing my best, no more and no less?

After _____, what can I do to leave the task behind and be present to the rest of my day?

REFLECT: NATURAL WONDERS

Think of one of the most impressive, spectacular places you could ever be. I find that natural wonders are most helpful, as nature gives us a much larger perspective of time and space than what we normally experience and think about.

Perhaps you have enjoyed many such places in your life. Imagine what you love about this place. Those things that you love also apply to you.

THINK: LIVING AS A SURVIVOR-THRIVER

When I began teaching, I had no real understanding of what I was doing at a junior high level. Of course, in retrospect, I can see that I was trying to save myself through saving kids who were at the same age and state of poverty and vulnerability that I was when I was abused. At the time, however, I saw that I was choosing to help kids and make the world a better place.

I was frustrated and often unhappy that I was working so hard and seeing few measurable results in my inner-city, gang-infested school. One day, a colleague shared with me that during her own first year of teaching at the school, she also felt burdened by the job and considered quitting many times. She said she eventually came to the realization that she didn't have to do this anymore if she didn't want to. Somehow, this helped me understand that no one was "making me" teach, get a credential, or teach where I decided to teach. Those were all part of my own choices.

As a teacher, like many teachers, I would give so much that I didn't take a restroom break. As silly as this might seem for a person who has healthy boundaries and practices self-care, this

was, for me, part of the job: to be so available to students all the time so that I was not able to take care of myself. I figured that this loss of private space and bathroom time was part of the teaching experience or that teachers just developed super-duper bladders.

A family friend, who was an administrator in L.A. Unified, suggested that I think about being an administrator, because he had known me my whole life and knew that I would want to do more and more things to help kids and influence schools. So I got my Master's degree at U.C.L.A. and began to work as an administrator.

And then when I was working as an assistant principal at a middle school, my supervisor suggested that I think about being a superintendent, because there are three power positions in a district: Superintendent, principal, and classroom teacher. I left that school to work as an administrator in a large high school, where I soon became miserable about many aspects of administration that were way beyond my control. Work took over my life and I saw less and less of my family. I felt that I was losing my soul.

Around that time, I heard a speaker raise the question, "If you suddenly won the lottery, what would you do and what would you never do again?" I made a list of what I would do: finish doctoral studies, create scholarships for students who wanted to somehow bring peace to the world. I started a list of what I never wanted to do again: never have to manage a high school football cross-town rivalry crowd again, which of course, followed a full day of work and was followed by supervising a dance, and all the behavior that enforcing those events entailed.

As an administrator, there were many things that I was very unhappy doing or that felt as though they made me a victim in some way. I worked tenaciously to keep up with everything, at the cost of self-care, because I assumed that these were part of the environment that had

chosen me to make a difference, to humanize and reform it. At that point of great tension between my loves, ideals, and responsibilities, I realized that I had a choice, and that I wasn't powerless over my career. I made the sacrifice in pay to begin teaching teachers, which was very meaningful for several years.

These are examples of choices, good and bad, that any of us can make at personal, interpersonal or professional levels. They may seem very limited if we see some things as "non-negotiable": salary, personalities, or particular items. Living as a Survivor-thriver means that we begin to understand that to the degree that we take things personally, we must also take responsibility for our lives.

ACT 3.11: CONSULTING WITH THE UNIVERSE

Answer the following questions with respect to any of your answers to the question, "What do I want?"

- How open am I to spending time with one more source to help me understand what the larger universe's intention might be for me regarding this desire?
- How about two or more sources?
- How easy is it for me to hear counsel, or do I struggle with what I hear?
- How willing am I to accept feedback or counsel that I may disagree with?
- When I receive counsel, how often do I find the need to take immediate action or can I wait?
- When I have taken action, how difficult is it to remain in the present and let go of my ideas of the action, past or future?
- When the outcome of my action is not what I initially desired, how well do I accept the outcome and appreciate or enjoy my participation in this process?

THINK: LETTING GO OF WHAT WE DON'T WANT

Imagine the most beautiful and valuable art piece you know of. Years ago, I spent a week in a remote town in the state of Chihuahua, Mexico, called Mata Ortiz. I worked with one of the master potters, who had been trained by Juan Quezada himself, the second citizen in Mexican history to be declared a national treasure for his restoration and expansion of the ancient Paquime pottery tradition. We collected clay from the riverbed, prepared it for use, built

the layers and formed, sanded, oiled, and then carefully painted the pots before firing them, all without electricity or other modern help. Our paintbrushes were fashioned from strands of hair from our own heads, just as they had been done hundreds of years ago with the Paquime Indians, which makes the extraordinary painting done by these potters even more impressive. I was surrounded by phenomenal artists. When I imagine precious art, I think of their works.

Religion, scripture studies, and theology, in my mind, are much like these exquisite works of art. Some people dedicate years of study, research, and focus to be experts in these fields, to be able to differentiate between real art and high or low-quality artistry, between authentic scriptural interpretation and misinformation. In our religious formation, we developed a world view through religious education; we came to associate great value with the teachings of these traditions. Perhaps they became as awesome or as precious as Michaelangelo's David or the Sistine Chapel or whatever your most valuable art piece is. These are breathtaking works of art.

The art piece may cost tens of thousands of dollars, even millions. Think of a Rembrandt or Van Gogh painting and appreciate the story of its creation, preservation, and brilliance. Let it inspire you and confirm that its maker was touched by God to have produced something so valuable, so extraordinary, so worth millions of dollars. Fall in love with it.

What if enlightenment, healing or deep happiness were inside the David? What if your salvation were on the other side of the Sistine Chapel and could only be reached by breaking through it? Would you do it? Is salvation so important that you would break what you have

held to be priceless, even touched by God? Rather than destroying a church, temple or people who worship where you were abused, I suggest letting them go if you desire happiness and peace.

I believe that happiness and peace following RASA are the by-products of reconciling our former abuse with the joys, desires and hopeful experiences and our own spiritual lives. My suffering, depression, and PTSD led me to an appreciation that I was spiritually dead, and that it was time to let go of the sentimentality or veneration of the religious traditions in which I had died. My difficult and painful mourning was the key that opened the door from my virtual death-row sentence to my spiritual release.

The difference between surviving and thriving (chapter 4) is when a person begins to see her choices and attachments, conscious and unconscious, as deeply related to her quality of life or to outcomes in personal or professional matters. Perhaps this means joining another church or temple where you find support and appreciation for your recovery and spiritual path. Perhaps it means detaching from external religious traditions and paying attention to your soul and spiritual life through meditation. Perhaps it means a combination of these paths. It certainly means choosing life.

ACT 3.12: HAVING WHAT YOU WANT

Given that you have tremendous power to influence your well-being, what are you willing to do to have what you want? On one hand, there is the idea that we don't have to do anything because whatever we currently have is exactly what we want. On the other hand, we can make our choices more active. If, therefore, you have some things that you want, pay attention to how it is that you have them. Do more of that. If there are some things in your life that you do not want, consider this your opportunity to make a change.

Review your list of answers to the question, "What do I want?" How many of the things that you put on your list are things that you currently have? What did you do to have them and what are you doing to continue having them?

As to the things that are on your list that you do not have, what are you willing to do to have them? In other words, what will you gain by doing those things? In one year, how will your life be different if you do those things? What is getting in the way or what is keeping you from doing those things?

Now, think of the opposite scenario. What will you lose? What will you and others lose if you do not do those things? In other words, in one year, what experiences or opportunities will have been lost to you if you do not do those things? In five years, what will you or others have lost if you do not make a change?

What do you commit to doing now in order to have more of what you want?

SECTION TWO
HOW DOES A SURVIVOR COME TO LIVE AT A LEVEL OF CHOICE?

"For every problem, there is one solution which is simple, neat and wrong."

"And ye shall know the truth, and the truth shall make you free."
John VII

"Ye shall know the truth, and the truth shall make you mad."
Aldous Huxley

"Vision without action is a daydream. Action without vision is a nightmare. "
Japanese Proverb

"Non est ad astra mollis e terris via."
(There is no easy road from the earth to the stars)
Seneca

"It was the Best of Times, It was the Worst of Times."
Charles Dickens

SURVIVOR-THRIVERS

THINK: DEEP LEARNING

Living at a level of choice requires seeing multiple perspectives, a talent that is sometimes developed through what many refer to as deep learning. This is the learning that takes place between familiar and new understanding. As victims, we may have paid most attention to what we were conscious of (Knowing what we Know or KK). We were split off from our unconscious and trauma. In a sense, we were unconsciously incompetent when it came to dealing with our abuse. As survivors, we may have begun to work with our toxic experience, and may have begun to learn more about our own and others' abuse than we ever imagined. This is like coming to Know what we Don't Know (K DK); in that stage, we might feel consciously incompetent, as the exercises in chapter 2 might have illustrated.

Survivor-thrivers enter into new psychological ground with respect to reconstructing our self-understanding, self-acceptance and self-development. This comes as a result of moving beyond the raw, reactive experiences of survivorhood and being willing to Not Know what we

Don't Know (DK DK).

In each shift from one stage to another, the experience and temporary consequence of deep learning is often marked by anxiety, frustration, and disequilibrium. The learner, once confident and competent in what was familiar or fairly simple, often feels deskilled, incompetent or inadequate. The experience might be one of going from a place of "not knowing", or Blind consciousness, to a place of Hidden consciousness. It may be from going from Private understanding to Public understanding. All shifts in consciousness push us between familiar and new understanding. The learning process may always bring feelings of being deskilled, incompetent or inadequate. However, survivor-thrivers act less from a place of Fight-Flight (victimhood) or Reactivity (survivorhood), and more from a place of mindful awareness or observation of their experiences.

Survivor-thrivers shift from living as surviving to living as choosing, willing to move forward through anxiety, frustration and disequilibrium into a deeper level of complexity and capacity to understand any problem and any solution in more and more ways. This is a critical and difficult step: choosing life and creating the futures we want. We don't forget our experiences of abuse, but we understand that we are more than our titles, positions or possessions. We know that we are more than our experiences, good and bad. We become liberated from our fears through the walking on new ground of self care: letting go of what is toxic and integrating our bodies, minds, and spirits.

ACT 3.20: SURVIVOR-THRIVER SIGNS OF HEALING

Write any examples that come to mind about yourself under any of these descriptors that you have seen in your own life.

It is through a courageous journey of healing that Survivor-thrivers:

...recognize what normal is when they see it.

...follow some projects through from beginning to end, and let go of others that are not appropriate to be undertaken at the time.

...reconcile their truth with others' truths.

...forgive themselves for judging themselves and others without mercy.

...have fun sometimes.

...love (not take) themselves seriously.

...work with the difficulties that come with intimate relationships.

...accept changes over which they have no control.

...welcome approval and affirmation.

...find connections with others even though they may behave differently than other people.

...are responsible for themselves.

...extend loyalty, except in the face of evidence that loyalty is undeserved.

... give serious consideration to alternative behaviors or possible consequences for a course of action.

...once involved in a plan of action, adjust as evidence develops and learn from their efforts, whether or not they resulted in the expected outcomes.

THINK: LIFE IMITATING ART

In the model below, I amplify discussions from the first two chapters and use some movie examples to describe how Survivor- thrivers are situated in various family, social or religious systems.

	Victim *The Wall*	Survivor *Pleasantville*	Survivor-thriver *Contact*	Thriver *Way of the Peaceful Warrior*
Individual	Individual is groomed/ exploited	Person experiences PTSD/ psychological splitting	Person reconciles past and present	Person shares healing

One scene from "The Wall" is particularly provocative with respect to this first column. The scene shows students portrayed as a faceless herd of cattle in cattle cars followed by another scene of students sitting in rows while the teacher berates the young boy. Suddenly, song lyrics blare, "We don't need no thought control, no dark sarcasm in the classroom — hey, teachers, leave those kids alone. All we are is just another brick in the wall."

The students, as mechanistic robots, march from an assembly line conveyor belt into a meat grinder, where their individuality, voice, talent, and spirit are destroyed. For this discussion, the faceless students represent children who eventually become victims of clergy sexual abuse. In such an environment, survivors might be represented by the rioting, destructive students who dismantle the classroom factory in the subsequent scene.

In "Pleasantville", the television viewers are sucked into TV-land, into a monocultural, monochromatic world. This "perfect world" is devoid of crime, poverty, sex and even bad weather as long as no one steps out of the normative talk or behavior. It is a world where Father knows best, where Mother cooks dinner, and where sibling small missteps are addressed with serious-but-kind lectures. Survivors, in this scenario, might be represented by characters in the movie who begin to question why things are the way they are and begin to feel their feelings. Survivor-thrivers might be represented by those in the story who embrace their newfound passions, and who make a conscious choice to stay or leave Pleasantville. In either case, they are never the same.

The films "Contact" and "Way of the Peaceful Warrior" illustrate the challenges and benefits of integrating previously unrecognized or valued aspects of ourselves into our day-to-day lives. "Contact" depicts an agnostic scientist who makes contact with life beyond her or others' scientific understanding. She suddenly lives with the frustration of telling her story regardless of how unbelievable it seems to others. She risks her professional loss of credibility by making her memories and experiences, over which she had

no control, public. She resists the temptation to minimize her experience or "shut up", in order to pacify others from her scientific community. Ultimately, she comes to accept and integrate her deep learning, which appears to be something like a marriage of science and faith, in a way that she could never reconcile in her previous self-perception.

Cesar Chavez once said, "Once social change begins, it cannot be reversed. You cannot uneducate the person who has learned to read. You cannot humiliate the person who feels pride. You cannot oppress the people who are not afraid anymore." This quote relates to the third column, which describes the process in which victim-survivors come to reconcile their experiences with their beliefs or current understanding. This process leads to the "deep learning" that I described earlier in the chapter.

A significant component to how Survivor-thrivers move forward in their healing and integration lies in their accepting coaching or mentoring from others, which helps them learn to navigate their environments. Ideally, survivors come in contact with a mentor who can walk with them as they integrate previously fragmented aspects of their identities, reconciling their conscious and unconscious selves, their egos and their shadows. As a result, Survivor- victims value critical thinking and seek understanding. They find various groups as arenas in which to learn and they become authors of their own lives.

"Way of the Peaceful Warrior" is the story of an Olympic-class college gymnast's recovery and transformation from a motorcycle accident that leaves his leg shattered. The main character experiences physical devastation, like "victimhood". Despite obvious physical devastation, he embarks upon a furious personal and physical struggle to rebuild his athletic career and return to his prior "normal" life, like "survivorhood". However, it is not until he submits to a spiritual mentor to accelerate his physical recovery that he discovers a spiritual, physical, and emotional revival and self-transcendence, like "Survivor-thriverhood". Eventually, he experiences a life of a thriver, integrated, and he is wiser than before.

ACT 3.21: RIGHTS

Survivor-thrivers develop the understanding that they have both rights and responsibilities related to their safety, health, and happiness. Many 12-step groups are useful for developing this understanding and capacity to practice living at a level of choice. The following "rights" reflect the kind of critical thinking that is promoted in 12-step support groups. To what degree do you believe them for yourself?

- You have numerous choices in your life beyond mere survival.
- You have the right to grieve over what you did not get that you needed or what you got that you did not want or need.
- You have a right to follow your own values and standards.
- You have the right to say no to anything when you feel you are not ready, safe or invalidated.
- You have a right to dignity and respect.
- You have a right to make decisions.
- You have a right to determine and honor your own priorities.
- You have the right to have your needs and wants respected by others.
- You have the right to terminate conversations with people who make you feel put down or humiliated.
- You have the right not to be responsible for others' behavior, actions, feelings, or problems.
- You have the right to make mistakes.
- You have the right to expect honesty from others.
- You have the right to your feelings.
- You have the right to be angry at someone you love.
- You have the right to be unique.
- You have the right to be scared and to say, "I am afraid."
- You have the right to let go of fear, shame and guilt.
- You have the right to change your mind at any time.
- You have the right to be happy. You can be healthier than those around you.
- You have the right to stability, "roots", and healthy relationships of your choosing.
- You have a right to your own personal space and time needs.
- You do not need to smile when you cry.
- You can be relaxed, playful and frivolous.
- You have the right to a peaceful environment.

Write what comes to mind as related to any of these descriptors that you have seen in your own life.

What do we have to gain by taking on some of these behaviors? What do we have to lose by taking on some of these behaviors?

I once heard Whoopi Goldberg tell a story about a woman who was remaking her life, and was walking to work to lose weight and meditate. Each day, she passed a pet shop along her way and heard a parrot shriek "You're fat!", seemingly to her. She continued and the parrot continued, "You're ugly!" She walked quickly past and sometimes crossed the street, but the parrot persisted, "You're fat! You're ugly!"

After a week of this, she confronted the owner, who agreed to put the parrot out of sight, but to no avail. When she neared the pet store, the parrot unleasheed its insults.

After another week of this, she served the pet store owner with an order to remove the parrot, silence it, or have it be put down for disturbing the peace.

The next day, the woman walked past the pet store slowly and the parrot was silent. On her way home, she walked past the pet store even more slowly, and the parrot made a sound like it was clearing its throat. She stopped and entered the store. The parrot made a throat-clearing sound again. She approached the parrot, the two staring each other in the eye. Finally, she was standing in front of the bird cage saying, "Well? Well? What have you got to say now?" The parrot twisted its head from one side to the other without saying a word. "Well? Well?"

The parrot cleared its throat one more time and said, "You know."

The transformation work described in this chapter is about people who are making strides and yet continue to wrestle with internalized, left-over voices that are in our heads, the ones that answer, "you know". We may attribute these voices or self-talk to something that we value or hate about our parents or the cultures that we grew up in. We can find that we reinforce the negative thinking that we hate and that if we are unhappy with our lives, we have chosen our unhappiness. Dr. David Simon, co-founder of the Chopra Center in La Costa, CA, offers the axiom, "to always get what you want, agree that what you have is what you want".

If you won the lottery tomorrow, how would that make you happy? Even if you paid all your bills or bought a new car or home, would you still have the voices in your head that reminded you of your unhappiness? Even if you didn't win the lottery, what is keeping you from letting go of your unhappiness and being happy?

SURVIVOR-THRIVERS

Section Three
What are some implications of living at a level of choice?

"The reason people blame things on previous generations is that there's only one other choice." **Doug Larson**

With rights come responsibilities. My experience of taking responsibility for my happiness has been greatly aided by wisdom and inspiration from folks like Thich Nhat Hahn, Deepak Chopra, and others. The following summary comes from *The Four Agreements,* by Don Miguel Ruiz. I have followed each agreement with a few of my favorite *dichos*, or folk sayings. In short, they are:

- Let your word be impeccable

- Don't take things personally

- Don't assume

- Do your best

THINK: Responsibility as Honesty

Be impeccable, honest with your word. This sounds simple enough, yet it is a very powerful standard to maintain. Keeping your word means many things: telling the truth; using your words in good ways; and not gossiping or exaggerating. Gossiping seems to make up much of the entertainment industry, as well as news shows. And gossip can be compared to a computer virus. Like a virus, gossip can cloud or poison our thinking and behavior toward others. Use your words to spread truth and love. Live up to your word. Don't hurt yourself or others with your word; play within the boundaries of your truth. Consider the following folk sayings:

- There is a great distance between said and done.

- Truth is God's daughter.

- They preach well who live well.

- A small spark makes a great fire.

ACT 3.30: Honestly

What can or will you do to live up to your word that will benefit you?

What can or will you do to live up to your word that will benefit others?

THINK: TAKING THINGS PERSONALLY

Don't take things personally. Projections are what people do when we split off a part of ourselves and then notice and respond positively or negatively to others when we see that trait in them. If I see you on the street and I say something negative, like, "You are so stupid", that's really a psychological projection. It is not about you; it's about me. So, even if someone criticizes your work or something you have done, don't take it personally. You're not your work, your accomplishments, or your failures. When you take things personally, then you feel offended, and your reaction is to defend your beliefs and add to the problem, whatever it may be. When you make it a strong habit to not take things personally, you avoid carrying the emotionally toxic reactions into your life. You are not responsible for the actions of others. You are responsible for you.

- No one has done good who has not suffered disillusionment.

- Those who recognize their folly are on the road to wisdom.

- One who plants a walnut tree does not expect to eat of the fruit.

- Even the best cloth has an uneven thread.

ACT 3.31: WITH DETACHMENT

What can or will you do to not take things personally so as to benefit yourself?

What can or will you do to not take things personally so as to benefit others?

THINK: ASSUMPTIONS

Don't make assumptions. We have the tendency to make assumptions about so many things. The problem with making assumptions is that we confuse them with truth. We could swear they are real. As the old saying goes, "When you assume, you make an **ass** out of **u** and **me** both." We make assumptions about what others are doing or thinking—we take it personally. We then blame them and react by sending out emotional poison with our words or reactions. When we make assumptions, we are asking for problems.

A common mistake we make is that we assume everyone sees life the way we do, thinks the way we think, feels the way we feel, etc. On the other hand, we might assume that others are so different that we have nothing in common. A simple and radical way to keep you from making assumptions is to ask questions. Have the courage to ask questions until you are as clear as you can be, and even then do not assume you know all there is to know about a given situation. Once you hear the answer, you will not have to make assumptions because you will know the truth.

- Faces of others we see, but not their hearts.
- The eyes believe their own evidence, the ears that of others.
- One who asks a question does not err easily.
- The wise person never says, "I did not think."

ACT 3.32: WITHOUT ASSUMPTIONS

What can or will you do to not make assumptions so as to benefit yourself?

What can or will you do to not make assumptions so as to benefit others?

THINK: YOUR BEST

Always do your best. Under any circumstance, do your best. No more and no less. But keep in mind that your best is never going to be the same from one moment to the next. You might be sick or tired, but if you always do your best, you won't judge yourself, and inflict guilt, blame, or self-punishment. Also, when you do your best, your reward is the action; you're not dependent on a paycheck or praise to be satisfied with your effort. Rewards will come, but you are not dependent on the reward.

It is difficult to always be honest. Just do your best. Don't expect that you will never take anything personally; just do your best. Don't expect that you will never make another assumption; do your best.

- Where there is no want of will, there will be no want of opportunity.

- Blood is inherited and virtue is acquired.

- Diligence is the mother of good fortune.

- Pray to God and hammer away.

ACT 3.33: YOUR BEST

What can or will you do to do your best so as to benefit yourself?

What can or will you do to do your best so as to benefit others?

Write what comes to mind related to any of these descriptors that you have seen in your own life.

What do we have to gain by taking on some of these behaviors? What do we have to lose by taking on some of these behaviors?

SURVIVOR-THRIVERS

These four agreements relate to a point I made at the beginning of this chapter. A characteristic of a survivor-thriver is working with coaching or mentoring from others, which helps in learning to navigate environments. In other words, our healing and transformation is all about relationships. Relationships are mirrors for us to better understand ourselves: what we hate and what we are attracted to. Deepak Chopra asks, "For those people we like, what is it about them (ourselves) that we want more of? For people we dislike, what might it be about ourselves that we deny in ourselves that we don't want to see?"

In the following section, I describe what I believe are manifestations of our recovery in relationships or ways that we work with others. I have added to the list from chapter 2 to include survivor-thriver applications, as I see them. I hope you will come up with your own insight into how to work with others from a level of hope and acceptance of your best efforts.

Give people more than they expect and do it cheerfully (Purpose or Agency).

Victims:	Stealing from others
Survivors:	Hording, giving to get
S-T:	Giving only to those we like

Don't believe all you hear, spend all you have or sleep all you want (Purpose or self-worth).

Victims:	Live addictive lifestyle; live self- or other destructive lifestyle
Survivors:	Live an excessive lifestyle; live a consumeristic lifestyle, buying what others are selling
S-T:	Live a flexibly bounded lifestyle; select satisfying activities

Never laugh at anyone's dream. People who don't have dreams don't have much (Self-worth or voice).

Victims:	Steal, crush, or compete with others' dreams
Survivors:	Follow others' dreams, rather than believing and sharing our dreams with others
S-T:	Dream and share dreams with others

Love deeply and passionately. You might get hurt but it's the only way to live life completely (Purpose).

Victims:	Abuse our own or others' minds, hearts, and bodies
Survivors:	Live to not get hurt or to not lose (control), rather than loving ourselves (mind, heart, and body)
S-T:	Love self (mind, heart, and body)

When someone asks you a question you don't want to answer, smile and ask, "Why do you want to know?" (Purpose or Voice)

Victims:	Debate or argue to win
Survivors:	Discuss or debate to learn or get more of something, rather than dialogue to understand, learn or join with
S-T:	Dialogue to understand, learn, join

Remember that great love and great achievements involve great risk (Purpose or self-worth).

Victims:	Live to please and not make mistakes
Survivors:	Live to "get it right", be good or recognized, rather than living to learn and learning to live
S-T:	Live to learn and learn to live

Remember the three R's: Respect for self; Respect for others; and responsibility for all your actions (Purpose or agency).

Victims:	Live from crisis to crisis
Survivors:	Live to navigate or beat the system
S-T:	Live and let live; four agreements: Let your word be impeccable, don't take things personally, don't assume, do your best

SURVIVOR–THRIVERS

Write what comes to mind related to any of these descriptors that you have seen in your own life.

What do we have to gain by taking on some of these behaviors? What do we have to lose by taking on some of these behaviors?

SURVIVOR-THRIVERS

THINK: ARCHETYPES

Many people who love me and want the best for me have pointed out that I often live in the world of ideas or metaphor-land. Lest the value of these ideas be lost in generalities, I revisit the discussion in chapter 2 using Caroline Myss' four basic archetypes: **child, victim, saboteur,** and **prostitute** and the hole in the sidewalk scenario to illustrate my adult spiritual life, which I mentioned at the beginning of the workbook.

In short, I lived for many years as an over-achiever, addicted to activity, disconnected from my abuse by my pastor, but driven

spiritually and intellectually to serve (day 1). Then, I began to critique the status quo of seminary and church without knowing exactly why. Eventually, the flashbacks came and clarified my dissatisfaction and rage (day 2). Then I wrestled with reconciling my experiences of trauma and abuse with my current reality. I began to let go of past ideas and battles in order to choose new experiences and paths (day 3). Finally, I am living a new part of my life, walking new ground. All the past has prepared me to work to end sexual abuse everywhere (day 4).

	Day 1	Day 2	Day 3	Day 4
Victim	Blindsided—fall into hole	Denial-- know hole is there and still fall in	Choice-- try to avoid and fall in; walk around	Intentionality-- Walk around hole
Child	Spiritual orphan or wounded child, followed by Newborn or 'born again' experience; Living on spiritual milk and honey (e.g., accepting 'Nativity story' literally)	My seminary years—engaging with God with emotion, ranging from disembodied spirit (infatuation) to challenge (hey, I'm talking to you)	Spiritual effort should yield one vision per day; spirituality as work, crusade or holy war; human person having a spiritual experience	Golden Child (in-spired or in-spirit; river flows in and around; spiritual person having a human experience; contemplative in action

	Day 1	Day 2	Day 3	Day 4
Sabateur	Innocent zeal/ naïvete that is out of sync with "status quo" at seminary; bringing in my experience and asking questions that others don't want to ask	Connecting with liberation theology, social and political activism; critique status quo for not doing enough or leave seminary and begin to teach	Leave church and education institutional life; return from abuse battlefield and take up public service	Facilitate national and international healing in service of ending CSA
Prostitute	"Betrayed by faith" - unable to share secret and shame; contracting spiritual cancer	Working with religious and secular institutions to do good, even though I felt used or compromised	I choose my partners, spiritually, intellectually, emotionally; Soul in body	Body in soul: promoting healing (integration of body, soul, and mind) by taking various roles

Similarly, *teaching* from a level of survival resulted in argument with authority figures, rather than discourse. At a level of choice, I built upon my teaching experiences with advanced studies and became a school administrator. I subsequently chose to continue studying and to earn my doctorate in Educational Leadership, which allowed me to teach teachers and engage with other teacher educators and educational policy makers.

In the early 1980s, when I was studying to be a priest, I felt drawn to a healing ministry. Over the subsequent years, I generally worked at my own happiness, but mostly chose to advocate for others' health and well being. More than twenty years after imagining myself as a healer, I began to work with healers to address my own woundedness. In addition, I have incorporated my experiences and understanding of systems in which members are either sexually or symbolically abused as a teacher-scholar.

The *artist-wizard* in me began to shift from telling others' stories to learning from writers and potters about telling my own story and paying attention to my own spirit and spiritual path. After my formal academic training, I took writing and pottery classes. At the same time, I began to reconnect with playing music, guitar, again, after having left it aside for several years. In the early 1980s, music had been a part of my ministry. It was a spiritual, emotional, creative way for me to understand myself and inspire others that I have revived in formal educational and religious settings.

	Day 1	Day 2	Day 3	Day 4
Teacher	Act or overachieve as good student	Argue vs. engage in thoughtful discourse	Teach teachers and engage with other teacher educators and educational policy makers	Share teaching ministry
Healer	Advocate for others' health and well being	Generally work at my own happiness	Work with healers to address my own woundedness	Share healing ministry
Artist/ wizard	Tell others' stories	Learn to tell my own story	Reconnect with playing and writing music	Share music ministry

Choose a period of your adult life and consider how you have acted according to the four days, according to the hole in the sidewalk scenario. Begin with the general categories below. If it is helpful, consider any of the core archetypes or other archetypes that you identify with, and add those reflections.

SURVIVOR-THRIVERS

	Day 1: Fall in	Day 2: "Accidentally" fall in	Day 3: Fall in for last time	Day 4: Walk around
Victim				
Child				
Saboteur				
Prostitute				
Other				

Section Four
What Can You Do?

"This is my simple religion. There is no need for temples; no need for complicated philosophy. Our own brain, our own heart is our temple; the philosophy is kindness."

— **The Dalai Lama**

You have a choice over the way you live. The way you change the way you live is to change the way you think about your life story: Change your relationship with your past and you will change your present and the future that is unfolding. In this way, you change the world around you by changing your worldview. Deepak Chopra talks about shifting from having an object-subject relationship with the world, or the world impacts me, to having a subject-subject relationship with the world, or I impact the world. Peter Block talks about taking back our projections of deficiencies and focusing on gifts.

THINK: Inner Life

The best way I know to take back and let go of negative projections is to tap into our inner life, our spiritual life. In this way, we begin to think and live as spiritual beings having a human experience. I found seminars from the Chopra Center, such as "Healing the Heart and Seduction of Spirit", to be invaluable in this process. Others have found other institutes to be transformative.

When not participating in formal programs of healing and personal transformation, meditation is invaluable. It helps you listen to and take care of yourself. It helps you manage your own boundaries and make healthy decisions because you are in touch with your best self. As adults, some of our choices are congruent with deeper values and some are incongruent with those deeper values. It may take years of bringing more and more areas of our lives together, in congruent or integral ways. This relates to "integrity", where things can be integrated. Living at a level of "choice", we may choose many fragmenting behaviors or make many fragmenting commitments, which may be individually good and collectively fragmenting. This is all under the umbrella of "choice".

Practice listening to yourself. Take time on a regular basis to be quiet and listen to your heart, soul, or core of your being. Use the following mantras as you practice sitting or walking meditation .

Breathing in, I calm my body.
Breathing out, I smile.
Dwelling in the present moment
I know this is a wonderful moment.

Thich Nhat Hahn writes, "To sit is not enough. We have to be at the same time. To be what? To be is to be a something, you cannot be a nothing. To eat, you have to eat something, you cannot just eat nothing. To be aware is to be aware of something. To be angry is to be angry at something. So to be is to be something, and that something is what is going on: in your body, in your mind, in your feelings, and in the world."

SURVIVOR-THRIVERS

ACT 3.40: MEDITATION EXPERIENCES

Use the following questions to the degree that they help you pay attention to yourself in meditation.

What emotions are arising within me?

What is occurring to trigger my emotions?

What do I need that I am not receiving? How can I take care of myself and ask for what is appropriate from another?

What am I getting out of not getting my needs met?

What do I really want? Am I really asking for what I want?

REFLECT: MANAGING YOUR OWN BOUNDARIES

Given the tasks or list of things that I have to do in the next 24 hours, how can I operate with full responsibility for my satisfaction? In other words, how can I leave or take a break, shift my expectations or find a new task or way of working so that my time is productive or satisfying? Given the things that I cannot literally walk away from, what is it that I am learning that will help me in this or a similar situation in the future?

THINK: MAKING HEALTHY DECISIONS

Survivor-thrivers have the good problem of discerning among many possible actions the best action to take. Ignatius of Loyola has been recognized for his criterion to help guide our actions when we might be torn between truths or good options, such as, "Which alternative will be more effective, more beneficial to, or more productive for myself and for others? Which alternative provides me with an opportunity to do good for myself and for my fellow human beings?"

- Stay in touch with reality and what is really going on. Pay attention to its concrete aspects, even to the small things.
- Develop an appropriate internal sense of timing. Do not act in too much haste, but do not drag out decisions either. Accept external time pressure as well as huge delays with prudence. Break down your decision-making process into steps and put them on a realistic timetable.
- Place your thoughts and plans before the critical eyes of your friends. Seek

the advice of prudent people. Examine your alternatives by testing them against experience.

- Listen to what your mind, your heart, and your intuitions tell you. Make sure all three of these voices from your soul are part of the final discernment; seek and trust simplicity.
- Know your limits; accept and observe them.

- Mourn the possibilities you ignored as well as the opportunities you missed. Your life is a path of letting go and dying.
- Once we are involved in the process of making a decision, we will reach a point where the "gordian knot" must be cut. We must accept the risks and let go.

ACT 3.41: HEALTHY DECISIONS

Write what comes to mind related to any of these descriptors that you have seen in your own life.

What do we have to gain by taking on some of these behaviors?

What do we have to lose by taking on some of these behaviors?

REFLECT: EVOLVING CONSCIOUSNESS

Einstein said, "No problem can be solved from the same consciousness that created it. We must learn to see the world anew." Deepak Chopra teaches that as we move from one state to another, we change. Our knowledge of ourselves and the world changes; our physical biology changes; our perception of what we see and hear, touch and taste changes; our cognition (what we know) and our feelings or moods change. Everything changes. He notes two key ideas of development throughout the states of consciousness: Knowledge is different in different states of consciousness, and reality is different in different states of consciousness.

Victim spirituality relates to "there and then" spirituality: We only really have what we've

been given to work with and we mourn that past. In other words, we have other people's interpretation of spiritual life, others' spiritual language, and others' spiritual truth. Survivor spirituality deals with "here and then" spirituality in that we do our best to apply other people's ideas, theology, and spiritual practices to our own current life. We may try anything to feel better and have a renewed sense of purpose and meaning.

Survivor-thriver spirituality is a here and now spirituality. It is perhaps the most difficult, as it is both letting go of preconceived notions and behaviors, as well as a discovering the vitality and power of the here and now. This here and now is a portal to other peak moments, past and future, which essentially and experientially deals with both-and practices. Our desire to move beyond the suffering forces us to trust in the present moments and makes use of our own spiritual instincts or desires. We're thrown back into being in our bodies, and by doing so, we may begin to experience meditation as being out of our bodies, in higher states of consciousness and connection to the universe around us. This is good.

The dis-embodiment that we felt as victims, the out-of-body experiences, the disassociation may be familiar to us, but now present themselves in self-directed and more intentional ways. We are teaching and learning as rooted in our own experiences of God in us. We are fashioning new skills that help us be connected with ourselves and that push us to find connections with others, at times in a frantic, accidental flurry of desperate isolation and at times in easy,

effortless union. We begin to understand Marion Williamson's counsel, "It's not just in some of us, it's in everyone. And as we let our own light shine, we unconsciously give other people permission to do the same. As we are liberated from our own fear, our presence automatically liberates others."

This chapter focused on the experiences and outcomes of integrating "victimhood" and "surivorhood", in what I have referred to as living as a Survivor-thriver. At the heart of being a Survivor-thriver is the reconciling of our previously split truths, our worst experiences and our best selves, and the transformation of them by living at a level of choice. To guide your work of integrating and reconciling your experiences and doing your best to do no harm to yourself, I recommend practicing the four agreements: Let your word be impeccable, don't take things personally, don't assume, do your best.

Share your thoughts on this book & possibly win prizes.
Everyone who shares ideas on how to make this workbook better
will get a free copy of the next edition of the book.
Go to www.HTSAH.com or www.HealingTheSexuallyAbusedHeart.com

CHAPTER FOUR
THRIVERS

INTRODUCTION

Chapter 1 was an introduction, and hopefully a distant review for many readers, as it dealt with living as a victim and dealing directly with the devastating victimization of religious authority sexual abuse. Chapter 2 described the difficult and very important work of moving from victim to survivor. Chapter 3 built on this past experience and growth to encourage personal healing: insight, skill development, and integration. In this chapter, we explore living as a thriver, a person who practices conscious living—what it means to walk around the holes in the sidewalk, or walk down another sidewalk in her life.

In this chapter, we will discuss thriving in many forms: living the four agreements, enjoying our present condition, laughing at our humanity with joy around our divinity, loving ourselves and others. Eckart Tolle speaks of this as the power of now. Other spiritual guides, among them Brother Lawrence, refer to being content in whatever situation they are in. Thriver living is marked by an articulation of simplicy from

complexity, a critical and compassionate understanding of self and others, and generativity or new thinking and new behaviors, a new heaven and a new earth. Thriver spirituality is marked by critical solidarity with others that leads others to their next level of learning or healing.

The power of presence in thrivers is palpable to others, and the impact of presence is inspiring. This is what I understand as relational power, or power through influence rather than force. The reader who has experienced thrivers has experienced people who are connected to or who articulate spirit, or "in-spiration". Listen to any number of Dr. Martin Luther King Jr.'s speeches, or others such as Bishop Desmond Tutu, Nelson Mandella, Rigoberta Menchu. Do you hear yourself in them? Your job as a thriver is to practice your self-worth wherever you go. You are part of the solution of your own and others' healing, as these extraordinary people are and have been.

THINK: LEAVING HOME

I'm off!
I must leave the political and ethical compromises that have corrupted the faith of my Jesus.
I must leave the stifling theology, the patriarchal structures.
I must leave the enduring prejudices based on our God-given humanity, the colour of my skin, my gender or how my sexual orientation is practiced.

I must leave the mentality that encourages anyone to think that our doctrines are unchangeable.
I must leave the belief of those who insist that our sacred texts are without error.
I must leave the God of miracle and magic.
I must leave the promises of certainty, the illusion of possessing the true faith.
I must leave behind the claims of being the

recipient of an unchallengeable revelation.
I must leave the neurotic religious desire to know that I am right, and to play at being God.
I must leave the claim that every other pathway to God is second-rate, that fellow Hindu searchers in India, Buddhists in China and Tibet, Muslims in the Middle East and the Jews of Israel are inadequate.
I must leave the pathway that tells me that all other directions will get me lost.
I must leave the certain claim that my Jesus is the only way to God for everyone.
I must leave the ultimate act of human folly that says it is.
I must leave the Church, my home.
I must leave behind my familiar creeds and faith-symbols.
I can no longer stay in an unliveable place.
I must move to a place where I can once again sing the Lord's song.

I must move to where my faith-tradition can be revived and live on.
I must move to a place where children don't tell me what I believe is unbelievable but tell me they can believe what I believe.
I must move to a place where they are not playing at moving the deck chairs on the decks of an ecclesiastical Titanic.
I can never leave the God experience.
I can never walk away from the doorway into the divine that I believe I have found in the one I call the Christ and acknowledge as "my Lord".
I must move to dangerous and religiously threatening places.
I must move to where there is no theism, but still God.
I'm off! But to where, God only knows.

— David Keighley, An English Anglican Priest

ACT 4.00: GUIDED MEDITATION

Deepak Chopra, in *Peace Is the Way: Bringing War and Violence to an End*, discusses how every day of the week can be part of a larger intentionality towards living in peace. Meditation is an essential component of living intentionally, like drinking clean water is an essential daily requirement for health. Take a theme a day and let it speak to your meditation and guide your actions that day. Be and do something concrete each day, however small, for peace.

Sunday: Being for Peace
Monday: Thinking for Peace
Tuesday: Feeling for Peace
Wednesday: Speaking for Peace
Thursday: Acting for Peace
Friday: Creating for Peace
Saturday: Sharing for Peace

THINK: WHAT IS MY CONTRIBUTION TO THE UNIVERSE?

The following thoughts from Presbyterian minister Frederick Buechner speak to the deep level of internal connection that thrivers need to realize in their best selves. His reflection helps consider the question, "What is my contribution to the universe?" If it is difficult to consider "God" in this discussion, substitute something else: the divine, the cosmos, cosmic consciousness, etc.

It comes from the Latin *vocare*, to call, and means the work a person is called to by

God. There are different kinds of voices calling you to all different kinds of work, and the problem is to find out which is the voice of God rather than of Society, say, or the Superego, or Self-Interest.

By and large a good rule of thumb for finding out is this. The kind of work God calls you to is the kind of work a) that you need most to do and b) that the world most needs to have done. If you really get a kick out of your work, you've presumably met requirement a, but if your work is writing TV deodorant commercials, the chances are you've missed requirement b. On the other hand, if your work is being a doctor in a leper colony, you've probably met requirement b, but if most of the time you're bored and depressed by it, the chances are you have not only bypassed a, but probably aren't helping your patients much either.

Neither the hair shirt nor the soft berth will do. The place God calls you to is the place where your deep gladness and the world's deep hunger meet.

In earlier chapters, I described recovery and healing service in terms giving blood. The victim receives the organ transplants or the blood transfusions in order to stabilize and be out of immediate danger. A survivor may think about giving blood at the point that she is healthy and stable enough to do so; a survivor-thriver may give blood occasionally, as long as her responsibilities to herself are taken care of. However, thrivers, by their own recovery or transformation process, are now in a special category of supporting others' recovery that is akin to having the rarest kind of blood, or love, that can assist people in earlier stages of deep suffering. Thrivers, by their ongoing development, reflect an important and different kind of healing potential, akin to being a kind of spiritual platelets or bone marrow. Thrivers have a responsibility and potential to reach out to abusers and abused in service and compassion.

One of these special callings will certainly be to forgive your abuser, primarily for your freedom and also as a witness of hope and transformation to others. Some thrivers may feel called to the special outreach or service of helping victims of any kind of abuse. Some thrivers may feel led to work with pedophiles or people who are so loyal or addicted to their illusions of religious authorities that they may have unkowningly perpetuated RASA. Whatever your service or contribution to the universe, it is not better than those survivors or survivor supporters who make a more generic contribution to peace and harmony in others' lives. In the bigger picture, each of us is like a string that works or plays at different frequencies. Each of us must be tuned to our own best selves, our sense of call, for us to come together in harmonic sound with one another.

Peter Block discusses that we often have cacophony instead of harmony in our world. It is that we conventionally think that our view of the world is based on history, events, evidence, and this pattern is treated as fact and is decisive. It is called fact, but it is only a collective memory, which in the glare of midday sun we might irreverently call fiction. If we are committed to a future distinct from the past, then we treat events as a matter of choice, and we call this context, not culture.

Thrivers begin to see the "other" as my creation and as an extension or template of how I see myself. This is the essence of being accountable, acting as an owner and creator of what exists in the world, including the light and dark corners of my own existence. It is the willingness to focus on what we can do in the face of whatever the world presents to us. Accountability does not project or deny; accountability is the willingness to see the whole picture that resides within, even what is not so pretty.

Thrivers, therefore, along with others who transcend the traditional stories of power, purpose, value, and voice, have the capacity to create a world we want to inhabit and to do it for all. If we saw others as another aspect of ourselves, we would welcome them into our midst. We would let them know that they belong with all their complexity. Differences, instead of being problems to solve, become a source of vitality. At these moments, we become owners, with the free will capable of creating the world we want to inhabit. We become citizens who are committed to the whole, whether that is a city block, a community, a nation, or the earth. The antithesis of being a citizen is the choice to be a consumer or a client, which is what put us into the situation in which we were abused by a religious authority in the first place.

The premise of being a thriver is that the whole universe is available to us as we move beyond our parochial understandings of ourselves and God. In this chapter, we discuss living intentionally, which is essentially linked to the first two questions, "Who am I?" and "What do I want?", but most directly related to the question, "What is my contribution or service to others?" As with previous exercises related to these core questions, the idea is for you to come up with as many answers as possible to the question, "What is my contribution to the universe or how can I serve others?" Pay attention to how these responses resonate with you and bring you joy to consider for yourself and your use of your time, talents, and resources.

What is my contribution to the universe or how can I serve others?

What is my contribution to the universe or how can I serve others?

What is my contribution to the universe or how can I serve others?

What is my contribution to the universe or how can I serve others?

What is my contribution to the universe or how can I serve others?

What is my contribution to the universe or how can I serve others?

What is my contribution to the universe or how can I serve others?

How do your dreams serve others? How do these dreams bring peace and well-being to you and to others?

How are you authorized to continue to learn and grow? How are you authorized to work on your behalf and on others' behalf?

Given what you love and what you love to do, what feedback are you getting from the universe about your efforts, For example, is it frustrating, validating, confusing? If it is negative feedback, are you looking for love —validation, affirmation, support— in all the wrong places?

SECTION ONE
WHAT IS LIVING INTENTIONALLY?

Living intentionally is living from a place of connection with our inner life, our best self, soul, or whatever we call it. I believe it is living with integrity or coherence among our heart, vision, and actions. I believe that living intentionally is rooted in the consciousness that we are not humans having a spiritual experience, but rather spiritual beings having a human experience!

I believe that living intentionally is related to the idea of self-transcendence, wherein our thoughts become things. Some do not ascribe to any particular spiritual tradition or language, but describe the law of attraction and the power of using our conscious thoughts. The docu-drama, *What the Bleep do We Know?* links what we have learned in quantum physics to illustrate how little we actually know and how with such little precision we have understood our daily experiences in our physical world. The authors point out that of the 400 billion bits of information present each second, humans are only

aware of 2,000. We now understand that we do not understand atoms, germs, energy, or the universe today as we once talked about those things.

In a previous discussion of deep learning, I mentioned a movement from being consciously competent to being unconsciously competent. Living intentionally is living with unconscious competency and connection to the unifying life force in and around each of us. Living intentionally is related to a level of letting go, and making the choice to let go at a more consciously competent and unconsciously competent manner. This is not a new idea. St. Francis of Assisi and Rama Krishna declared in similar terms, "I am the machine and you, O Lord, are the operator. I am the house and you, O Lord, are the indweller. I am the chariot and you, O Lord, are the driver. I move as you make me move; I speak as you make me speak."

THRIVERS

THINK: CONTEMPLATING IN ACTION

Traditional contemplative prayer and meditation are not so much a way to find God as a way of resting in God whom we have found, who loves us, who is near to us, who draws us to unity. Yet, this is not a religious or particular ideological dogma, which may be criticized as mind control. The field of living intentionally is what I described as the large field of DK DK, where *we do not know what we do not know.* Contemplating in action means working with the unknown in and around us (the spirit or unifying field) and acting on behalf of that spirit. Contemplating in action recalls the state of transcendental consciousness that is reflected in poems and koans like "I do not know whether I was then a man dreaming I was a butterfly, or whether I am now a butterfly dreaming I am a man", by Chang-tzu; or Walt Whitman's, "I cannot be awake for nothing looks to me as it did before, Or else I am awake for the first time, and all before has been a mean sleep." Thrivers

are essentially contemplating in action, as the new ground of soul leads them to care for themselves and work with others differently. Earlier, I named Nelson Mandella, Rigoberta Manchu, and Bishop Desmond Tutu as thrivers. I believe that their actions, following the suffering and transformation they experienced, illustrate the saying by Arthur C. Clarke, "It may be that our role on this planet is not to worship God, but to create him."

They could have done what popular wisdom suggests and "shoot first and ask questions later", and continue our struggle as the species that controls nature or others. Instead, they are examples of the rightness of "survival of the wisest" as the evolution beyond survival of the fittest. They point us to work with our own authority, to claim it with respect and consideration of the present moment, and to co-create our future. For those contemplating in action, there are no random events, nor are there events in isolation. People who are contemplating in action begin to connect the dots and move in a flow of life, which is always now, in the present moment. Those who are contemplating in action understand the illusion of stars and see the self as consciousness, not as possessions or positions.

Meditation is one form of connecting with the vast depth of space in ourselves. We are both-and, both in one another and ourselves. We are subject-object consciousness shifting to subject-subject consciousness. This is the peace of God. This moves our collective lives to the next stage of our collective evolution of humanity, our contribution to the universe, ending child abuse, promoting universal love, happiness, etc.

ACT 4.10: THE PROMISES

I find the following adapted "12 Promises" to be accurate descriptors of the experiences related to living intentionally. Write what comes to mind related to any of these descriptors that you have seen in your own life.

1. We are going to know a new freedom and a new happiness.
2. We will not regret the past nor wish to shut the door on it.
3. We will comprehend the word "serenity".
4. We will know trust and peace.
5. No matter how far down the scale we have gone, we will see how our experience can benefit others.
6. That feeling of uselessness, powerlessness, hopelessness, and meaninglessness will disappear.
7. We will lose interest in rescuing or attacking others and regain our boundaries and take appropriate interest in our fellows.
8. Self-loathing will slip away.
9. Our whole attitude and outlook upon life will change.
10. Fear of people and of economic insecurity will leave us.
11. We will intuitively know how to handle situations which used to baffle us.
12. We will suddenly realize that God is doing for us what we could not do for ourselves.

What do you have to gain by taking on some of these behaviors?

What do you have to lose by taking on some of these behaviors?

SECTION TWO
HOW DO WE LIVE INTENTIONALLY?

How do we live a redeemed, transformed, or transcendent life? As a person who has experienced the toxicity of child sexual abuse, I know the path of victim, survivor, and survivor-thriver. I can attest to the practice of intentionality.

My experience of how to live intentionally is related to my practice of meditation. I believe that the two are interrelated. I also assume that the reader has begun a spiritual practice of her own at this point in the workbook.

In meditation, there is an experiential guideline: If you're trying, you're trying too hard. This doesn't mean that we don't work or have an active and dedicated practice to live our purpose. To me, it means that my flow of thinking and doing can merge with a larger flow of Spirit. Some might call it the collective unconscious. Some might call it the collective soul. The point is to pay attention and join soul with the role we take up as we make our contributions to the universe.

THINK: INTENTIONALITY IN PRACTICE

Deepak Chopra describes a sequence of spiritual practices for living with intentionality that is somewhat counter-intuitive to our culture of conquest, aggression, and ego. He describes some aspects of meditation and living that connect us with intention.

First: Silence.
As long as there is turbulence in the internal dialogue, we'll never get to the soul. Some practice Transcendental Meditation; others use a mantra. The practice of being still is no small matter.

Second: Surrender.
Jacque Maritain says, "Do not panic during painful times, nor look for the quick, easy solution, seeking a premature resolution of tensions. It is only by learning to live with tension that we Give God time to work … time to transform us into compassionate, forgiving, wise and loving people. It is when we allow ourselves to make a leap of faith into the uncertainty of the Unknown, that we discover Presence." When we let go of our idea that we have the big picture, we no longer have a need to control, manipulate, cajole, convince, beg, demand or seduce others or God as we imagine God.

Third: Being.
From surrender comes being. In silence and surrender, we access our life force as human beings, rather than as human doings. This ground is also the ultimate ground of every other being. Being in touch with this Being puts us in touch with the life force that connects all beings.

Fourth: Vision.
The Little Prince tells us, "It is only with the heart that one can see rightly; what is essential is invisible to the eye." Beyond bits of sensory experience, we can only believe, not see. In a sense, we believe a lie by believing in the fragments of information or perception we receive. Seeing from our deepest self, being connected with our universal life force, means to see the whole and participate in our wholeness, our holiness, and our healing.

Fifth: Intention.
In this wholeness, I see that my intent is also the intent of God and of the universe. This intention makes what may seem logically impossible possible: bumblebees fly; birds talk; victims forgive. In that intentionality, we are powerful and connected to the universe, and yet bounded.

Sixth: Action.
From our connection to God's life force, God's intention, we can "Ask and it will be given." In that place of asking, we experience right action. One description of this right action is, "By their fruit, they shall be known." This kind of action comes from a detachment from our ego. In a sense, it is transcendece of our ego.

THRIVERS

The following may be asked in general, and are offered as introductory questions to bring into your meditation practice.

What is the gift that you currently hold in exile?

What forgiveness are you withholding?

What is a commitment or decision that you have changed your mind about?

What resentment do you hold that no one knows about?

What is the positive feedback you receive that still surprises you?

THINK: SPIRITUAL MENOPAUSE

THRIVERS

I listened to a radio program recently by Dr. Christiane Northrup (*The Wisdom of Menopause*) wherein she discussed stages of women's health, and sustaining a healthy lifestyle of care-giving that includes the care giver. She used various examples of how women, through birthing and childcare, practice great self-sacrifice, which leads to poor health. Such examples of self-sacrifice are: getting a college degree that you don't like; going along with someone else's plan or vacation that you don't like; leaving a relationship that is bad for the woman and feeling bad for leaving.

In the introduction of this workbook, I referred to the cocoon and its metamorphosis process, which reminds me of her discussion of something of which I am ignorant: menopause. She referred to an emotional kind of ovulation and how there is a time to give up the full moon of your life. This means giving up what women have wanted to be perfect — office, house, etc; re-framing selfish, to include self-care; and asking for help, as in we're here to serve, but not meant to be the main course. She said that we must be willing to give up the life we had planned to have for the life that is waiting for us.

She described that FSH and LH hormone levels go up with respect to the ovulation cycle, maximizing receptivity to ideas and generativity, and that FSH and LH hormone levels go down with respect to the menstrual cycle. What she emphasized was that in peri-menopausal women, the FHS and LHS stay up. I don't know about that. I do know that her discussion resonated with me, as a man, with respect to spiritual development. What I particularly like about this analogy is that Dr. Northrup's discussion transforms the ways women and men can appreciate and value menopause, just as I am suggesting that people who have been victims can realize a new and extraordinary spiritual life.

The chapter discussions in this workbook might be thought of as related to a life cycle, a spiritual life cycle. Chapters 1 and 2 might describe the sickness that goes along with pregnancy. At times, a victim or survivor can feel sick with the changes of chemistry and mood, which can lead to confused self-understanding and evaluation by others who may not know or care about the process going on in us. Chapter 3 relates to the understanding that there is something special going on inside us that only we can bring forward. There are times that consultation with others helps us in the process of birthing this person inside us, our own Golden Child, if you will. Living intentionally involves taking time daily to gestate our new life and nurture our own best self. Meditation and other acts are ways to treat our best self as we have treated others. Meditation, at this point, can lead to an extraordinary spiritual quality of life that may never have been appreciated before.

I offer the following questions as resources to bring into your meditation practice.

What are the crossroads you face at this time?

What declarations are you prepared to make about the possibilities for the future?

What are your doubts and reservations?

THRIVERS

What is the "yes" you no longer mean?

What gifts are you receiving from the universe as you practice meditation?

SECTION THREE
WHAT ARE THE IMPLICATIONS OF LIVING INTENTIONALLY?

Gandhi said, "Be the change you want to see in the world." His life is a testament to living the steps of silence, surrender, being, vision, intention and action. Nelson Mandela transcended his imprisonment to lead South Africa towards reconciliation and social transformation. Many people live intentional and transforming lives throughout the world in big and in small ways. Each of us can promote reconciliation and transformation in the world, building bridges and roads as we move forward.

THINK: BEING A WOUNDED HEALER

I began teaching as a way to live and act as a warrior on behalf of poor and minority inner-city students. When it was time to teach about World War II, I invited a veteran from the Fighting 442nd Regimental Combat Team, the most decorated unit in U.S. military history. It was made up of Japanese-Americans who had been put into internment camps. This gentleman had been relocated to Manzanar. He talked from his experience about what it meant for him to wear the uniform, live and work in this country. He was inspiring.

I spoke with him afterwards and asked, "How can you be so positive about the country that treated you so badly? How can you be such a positive representative of the military and this government?" He said, "We have to forgive. We have to work with the folks who have power." I was coming from a place of militancy and he was coming from a place of deep compassion.

A few years ago, I visited Acoma Pueblo, the longest continuously inhabited community in the United States. The tour guide explained that the Acoma Pueblo Indians had been forced into labor, and had had to cut down and carry trees from a forest forty miles away for use building the church on the mesa. He pointed out that if a tree touched the ground, the Indians were beaten and sent back for a new tree, because the tree had been defiled. He talked about Don Juan de Oñate, who had ordered that the right foot of the Indian men be cut off, in a show of power. He later talked about the local inhabitants' practice of indigenous traditions as well as Catholic religious practices. I spoke with him

afterwards and asked how he could continue to practice religious traditions that had been so colonizing, so hostile and abusive. He said, "Out of respect."

Both of these people spoke with deep sincerity and with what I experienced as a sense of grounded identity. At the time, I was not consciously dealing with my repressed rage about my own exploitation. I was not cognizant about my own depression related to the loss of my own identity to the degree that I came to realize in 2002.

As my memories and activism increased, I never thought that I would speak with what might be a similar state of mind to say that "we have to work with abusers". At other times in my life, I have been immersed in non-violence, in a life of monastic reflection and prayer. I have treasured spiritual growth above everything. I knew the words related to forgiveness. I understood the value of forgiveness. At the same time, I never considered that I would one day be offering support to a registered sex offender who wanted to be part of the same church in which I have found my own spiritual rebirth.

In early 2007, the pastor called me and shared a hypothetical scenario wherein a registered sex offender might want to attend the church. He asked me how I would feel about it. I told him that I didn't know and that I was filled with lots of emotions, and would have to somehow reconcile that reality with my own experiences. The next time the pastor called me, he asked if

THRIVERS

I would be part of a spiritual support team that would work with this person until a decision could be reached about this person's participation in the church. The church membership at large had begun a volatile and painful process of voicing its concerns, beliefs, and experiences related to sexual abuse. Some who had repressed their own sexual abuse for many years felt re-victimized by the mere thought that a registered sex offender would be allowed to worship in the place that they had perceived as a refuge of safety and comfort for so long.

I reluctantly agreed because this pastor was the first religious authority who offered no defensiveness or shame as I brought my pain from sexual abuse to him. I trusted him and I knew in my heart of hearts that I would need to be a resource for anyone who had suffered sexual abuse. Having been a public advocate for reconciliation, honesty, and disclosure of documents related to pedophile clergy, I knew that I would need to be part of the solution and reconciliation process.

A couple of weeks later, I sat in a room with the support group and the registered sex offender. Those meetings over the next several months led to breakthrough experiences for me, and have become life-changing in my own metamorphosis.

ACT 4.30: RESPONDING TO THE INVITATION

The experience of working with a registered sex offender prompted me to write the following to other sexual abuse victim advocates across the country. We shared an interest in ending child sexual abuse and in transforming the practices in any religious group that perpetuate child abuse, but disagreed on how to move beyond the stance of confrontation and protest. Please read the following letter and answer the questions at the end.

Some recent difficult and positive experiences have really gotten me to this point of making a consultation about the roles that survivors take up in service of our own healing, and our effectiveness in helping others.

I think that it's futile (and maybe counterproductive) for survivors to continue to talk about any organization in which we find abusers and conspirators, as a personal issue. I don't think that it matters if the bishops 'get it' or care or have the capacity to respond meaningfully to survivors. It may be true that the bishops feel something that they and others experience or believe as heartfelt sorrow. It doesn't matter, really.

I'm coming to believe that I have been naïve in the past— knocking myself out to leaflet and get face to face with the average parishioner coming out of church, as if I might make child sexual abuse personal for her or him. I think those actions really only allowed these folks to be upset at me or you or other survivors, instead of their bishop— or to hold onto their own fantasy that a few bad religious authorities behaved badly. I think that the real work will happen when registered sex offenders show up and announce that they want to be ministered to, that they want to bring their contrite and messed-up selves to church.

My naiveté was to think that bishops, as representatives of a tradition and identity that for centuries has been about protecting assets (property, power, perception or image) over protecting kids, that for centuries has formally promoted secrecy, that for centuries has allowed abuse, could do anything different than live in and protect their castles, bubbles or empires. I was naïve to think that it mattered if these folks or faithful parishioners cared or not. All that was me taking and interpreting this abuse, this current moral bankruptcy, and diocesan self-protection as personal.

I know it's important for someone (it has almost always been survivors) to pound the doors and demand that the documents are released. I know that it's important for lots of folks to raise awareness about child sexual abuse, particularly by religious authorities. My experience, however, is that the more I do that, the more stuck and fragmented I feel. I think that my colleagues, students, and evaluators may have interpreted the symptoms I experienced from such activity as a kind of incompetence. I'm sure that my loved ones have experienced me as not being present, available, or responsible (i.e., able to respond).

I think that survivors will be called on to 'minister' to others by being compassionate teachers when the dams break. I think that there will be a time (soon) when there's more information than people can handle or deny about perps in parishes, and then lots of folks will become unglued. I think that when the first bishop washes away in a river of criminal charges and prison sentences, more dependent and naïve parishioners will feel lost and will gather to support one another, vent, and eventually listen to survivors. I think that at that time survivors need to be able to join in this larger healing process by sharing, not debating, with people who are trying to understand how the abuse and cover up happened.

I think that taking this whole abuse issue personally is a natural and 'beginning' starting point for us. But I think that survivors have taken up that stance or role and that we can do more as we let go of this 'personal' reaction.

Here is a case in point. My experience with my current, little church is that when a registered sex offender (who had been received under 'covenant of limited access' in another church) came to my little church, folks who hadn't dealt with their own abuse came unglued. Some recognized the fear or hysteria around the known registered sex offender as being related to their own life experiences. Most seemed to just react. A very skilled psychologist spent an initial open forum session with several church members and noted that many current conflicts or problems that he sees in couples' therapy are ten percent current issues and 90 percent old issues that are triggered by a current event or problem. Ninety percent.

I am currently in the 'covenant team' in my church that is dealing with how to accept a known perp. It is a difficult and, I think, necessary part of my own healing. I'm not accepting a role of sponsor. I'm in the room, bringing what I've learned, resources I have, and my voice.

I've participated in some larger group discussions about admitting this person into the congregation. I've been able to offer support to folks who are just dealing with their abuse as a result of this known perp showing up and asking to be a part of their previously 'safe' church or home. Now that other folks are taking this whole issue personally, we're planning real discussions and educational programs.

I really think that survivors need to tell their story in safe settings and in settings that are intended to be heard in a personal way (i.e., in a closed meeting and not on the news). I think that the invitation isn't there because the average person, who can be an ally and invite survivors to heal through telling their story, is covering her/his own trauma or hasn't woken up to the historic, systemic deceit. I think that the opportunity might come when an ordinary perp becomes known and people take it personally, and come unglued, and NEED to work through their blindness or naiveté that protects them from their own 90 percent.

My current church and others are struggling with KNOWN pedophiles. There are many abusers are out there that people don't know about and won't know about while the public discourse is 'all about the money'. However, as cases 'settle' and documents and videos are

THRIVERS

available, then I think that the next stage of this very important work will require a very different set of skills and behaviors from everyone. I suggest that survivors do whatever we can to get to a point where we can be and stay healthy in order to help others get healthy when they wake up.

I'll keep you posted on what I learn. Peace.

Write what comes to mind related to any of the points or descriptors that you read in the letter to survivor leaders and thrivers.

How have you seen points of the letter play out in your own life?

What would you do if something similar happened in your current organization, church, or temple?

THRIVERS

THINK: Thriver Implications

What follows is a comparison of possible manifestations of the same actions from a Survivor-Thriver and Thriver perspective. After each comparison, I have made a connection to various archetypes to help me understand actions that are relevant for me. Take a moment to link the comparison to your own actions.

Give people more than they expect and do it cheerfully.
S-T: Giving to those we like
Thrivers: Giving to those we don't like

For me, the healthier my child archetype is relates to how I can manifest this aspect. Eric Fromm said, "Not he who has much is rich, but he who gives much." A Thriver practices interdependence. How does your contribution to the universe relate to the descriptors above?

Don't believe all you hear, spend all you

have or sleep all you want.
S-T: Flexibly bounded lifestyle
Thrivers: Embodied spirit or Contemplating in action

I can readily use my experience as a Victim to see how I might create my own unhappiness. Miss Piggy might say, "Never eat more than you can lift." Tich Nhat Hahn might counsel us to breathe with intentionality, responding to our bodies and subsequently to others and our environment. How does your boundary management relate to the descriptors above?

Never laugh at anyone's dream. People who don't have dreams don't have much.
S-T: Dream and share dreams with others
Thrivers: Live and create dreams

Because I have hope, I have dreams. I would

not be a wizard without dreams. Earlier in the chapter, I included the quote, "I do not know whether I was then a man dreaming I was a butterfly, or whether I am now a butterfly dreaming I am a man." Even the nursery rhyme speaks to living as a Thriver: "Merrily, merrily, merrily, merrily, life is but a dream." Albert Einstein said, "When I examine myself and my methods of thought, I come to the conclusion that the gift of fantasy has meant more to me than my talent for absorbing positive knowledge." How does your contribution to the universe relate to the descriptors above?

Love deeply and passionately. You might get hurt but it's the only way to live life completely.

S-T:	Love self, mind, heart, and body
Thrivers:	Love others, mind, heart, and body

With some thoughtfulness, passion yields compassion. In my experience, I cannot expect to function as a healer if I do not care for those with whom I am working. Because I know what it is like to be sick, I can speak with authority about the benefits to me of being healthy. How does your contribution to the universe relate to the descriptors above?

When someone asks you a question you don't want to answer, smile and ask, "Why do you want to know?"

S-T:	Dialogue to understand, learn, and join
Thrivers:	Dialogue to teach; ask questions that help you understand and connect with others

I am blessed to be a teacher. Many people think of teaching as talking and learning as listening. In reality, deep learning turns that idea on its head. Transforming and powerful teaching are essentially linked to listening, and transforming and powerful learning are essentially linked to

talking and application. By understanding the context of the question, I can better field the question. This is what I think of with the saying, "If fate throws a knife at you, there are two ways of catching it: by the blade or by the handle." How does your contribution to the universe relate to the descriptors above?

Remember that great love and great achievements involve great risk.

S-T:	Live to learn and learn to live
Thrivers:	Learn to teach and teach to create

Ben Franklin said, "Any fool can criticize, condemn, and complain, and most fools do." I believe that it is normal to be a competitive or a saboteur at times. However, a Thriver takes that knowledge and applies it in a way that is deconstructive and reconstructive. How does your contribution to the universe relate to the descriptors above?

Remember the three R's: Respect for self; Respect for others; and responsibility for all your actions.

S-T:	Live and let live; four agreements: Let your word be impeccable, don't take things personally, don't assume, do your best
Thrivers:	Be the change you want to see in the world

Jesus ate with sinners, like the prostitute. He appeared to have managed his boundaries and have integrated his spiritual and sexual wholeness. In terms of wholeness or holiness, a saint has a past and a sinner has a future. My own experience is that my health care is now similar to an era in which I was very spiritually focused. My change of diet and activity is linked to my renewed focus on self-management, health and happiness. How does your contribution to the universe relate to the descriptors above?

THRIVERS

ACT 4.31: New Directions

Write what comes to mind related to any of these descriptors that you have seen in your own life.

What is the new path or direction for you?

What do you have to gain by taking on some of these behaviors? What do you have to lose by taking on some of these behaviors?

THINK: Healing Insights

Spiritual bliss is something that I enjoyed many years ago, during a time following a "conversion experience". It has been many years since I have felt like I am a spiritual person having a human experience or would ascribe anything like spiritual bliss to my experience. However, being still and practicing meditation has revived my entire life, even as I have learned through my experiences of "Victimhood", "Survivorhood", and "Survivor-Thriverhood". The following healing insights came to me through a healer, who has been helpful in my own recovery. I offer them as a prayer for you, the reader:

Part of your new freedom and happiness is going to be you being willing to let go of taking things personally, feeling that you're the victim, the person who's being abused in the situation. Once it becomes personal, then all those emotions get stirred up and blended together. I'm asking you to release that personal part of it. You have suffered. You have been abused. All that is true. If you can, it's time to let it go and see that it's not an us and them' situation. We're all in this together.

Start cutting away the past: suffering, pain, trauma, confusion. Decide to let it go. Call in forgiveness, not excusing what happened but letting it go so that you can go on, so that all the people you work with can go on and not get stuck in the past anger, the past 'victimhood'. Release the past and let it go.

Live in the present. It is safe to be present.

This idea of being free may feel scary to you. It's a new way of being and of being in the world. Maybe it means fear of becoming complacent and taking it easy. Perhaps it brings fear of separation in your relationships. Maybe it means fear of not fighting any more or perhaps that being free will corrupt you.

The corruption that's going on is about all of us. There are no winners and losers. We're all it, and the system needs to change so that everyone is respected and treated fairly and treated with kindness and love. If that doesn't happen, we all lose. It's not us and them. Healing is about all of us.

You're safe, you're safe, you're safe. Safe to be in your power, safe to be free. It's safe to express your power, safe to express your creativity. It's safe to voice your concerns, safe to be a minister. It's safe to be a representative of God.

Imagine that you're coming off of the battlefield. You're safe; you're free. You're no longer a mercenary in somebody's army. This life is your own.

It's safe for all these different parts of you: your understanding, your intuition, your power, your maleness, your spiritual aspects, and your ministry. You're a teacher, a healer, a fighter, a soldier, a golden child, a compassionate being. We ask that all these pieces of you be healed. We ask that they be allies— that they work together and be integrated into your being, into your nervous system, so that all these diverse skills and talents may work together.

The war inside is over. Peace has been declared throughout the land. Peace has been declared in your heart. It's safe to be at peace within yourself. By God's grace I call in peace: peace in your heart, peace in your soul, in all parts of you. Peace in your spirit.

ACT 4.32: LISTENING

Let these words soak into your mind and heart. Let them speak to you as truly as they speak to your neighbor, even to those who know not what they do, and who have brought harm to you or those you care for. Share these words in your actions, bringing peace in your heart, in your soul, in all parts of you wherever you go.

THRIVERS

SECTION FOUR
WHAT CAN YOU DO?

THINK: BE FULLY ALIVE

Iraneus, in the 2nd Century, said that the glory of God is you fully alive. Be fully alive! You've accumulated a lot of wisdom, a lot of experience and knowing how to handle power, how to wield power, how to hold power, how to share power, how to empower others. Be powerful!

The message that I have for you is that you need to ask for what you want. You need to be honest with yourself and with others; and if others don't want to give you what you want from them, that's fine, but at least you have to ask for it. You have to negotiate. But anything you haven't been asking for in your relationships, you have to ask, not as a demand, but just as a request. Trust yourself and let others hear that. Be purposeful.

It is time to know that you're the master of your own creation, and that all the things that have

happened in your life are there for you to learn, to grow, and to expand. And now, you can choose whatever it is that you want in your life. You get to be the creator, or at least the co-creator, of this life. Be fruitful.

It's safe, it's safe, it's safe for you to come into your power, for you to be fully awake, for you to be fully aware, for you to be great. It's safe, it's safe, it's safe to be a son or daughter of God, and to share that power and grace. It's all about how spirit comes into your life and what you do with it and how you share that and how it spreads into your relationships. Be helpful.

It is safe to embrace your own power. You're going to make some mistakes with it. That's okay. Be fully alive!

THRIVERS

ACT 4.40: PAY ATTENTION

Pay attention to your interactions with others. When you find yourself in a misunderstanding or you find yourself in what seems to be a relapse of sorts into "survivor" mode, allow yourself to laugh at the misunderstanding. Did you miss information or forget something that someone said, etc.? Is this a sign of being overloaded? This is normal, something that highly functioning people experience. As a Thriver, this is an opportunity to more quickly recognize the experience for what it is: a temporary bit of feedback that you are on overload and that you should make adjustments accordingly. Let it go. Move on.

ACT 4.41: BE THE CHANGE

There are many quick and simple actions you can take to prevent future abuse, help already wounded survivors to heal, and help those who are prisoners of their own beliefs or religious denial. The work of ending child sexual abuse is not limited to any religious group or gender. I think that the best thing for the reader to do at this point is to practice being present to yourself. Practice nurturing to your health in various aspects. While there are many possible actions that each person can take individually and collectively, I expect that you can reflect or meditate upon the following questions daily and you will find what is right for you and others.

Who am I?

What do I want?

What is or may be my contribution to helping the world be a better place?

REFLECT: LET YOUR LIGHT SHINE

Living as a Survivor or Survivor-Thriver can prompt us to act as if "when we do this, whatever this is, then we'll have this, then we'll be happy". Thrivers appear to practice a more grounded process of living and acting: Silence, surrender, being, seeing, intent, action, and fruit.

We can be co-creators of our own destiny. We can all develop intellectually, emotionally, and spiritually. You are authorized to continue to learn and grow. You are authorized to work on your behalf and on others' behalf. As Rev. Buechner observed, "Neither the hair shirt nor the soft berth will do. The place God calls you to is the place where your deep gladness and the world's deep hunger meet."

Thrivers, by their ongoing development, reflect an important and different kind of healing potential, akin to being a kind of spiritual platelets or bone marrow. Thrivers have a responsibility and potential to reach out to abusers and abused in service and compassion. Whatever your service or contribution to the universe, it is not better than those survivors or survivor supporters who make a more generic contribution to peace and harmony in others' lives. I believe that you will let your word be impeccable, that you will stop taking things personally, that you won't assume, and that you will do your best. I believe you will never leave the God experience, as you can never walk away from the doorway into the divine that is in you. I believe you must move to dangerous and religiously threatening places, to where there is no theism, but still God. I believe that "as we let our own light shine, we unconsciously give other people permission to do the same. As we are liberated from our own fear, our presence automatically liberates others."

Share your thoughts on this book & possibly win prizes.
Everyone who shares ideas on how to make this workbook better
will get a free copy of the next edition of the book.
Go to www.HTSAH.com or www.HealingTheSexuallyAbusedHeart.com

PART TWO

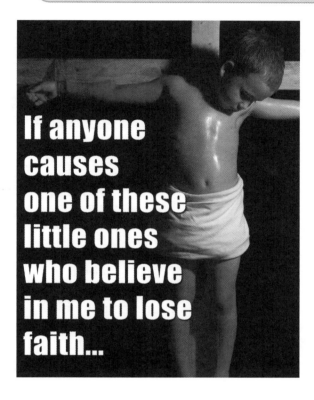

If anyone causes one of these little ones who believe in me to lose faith...

It is better that scandals arise than truth be silenced.

-St. Gregory

Our Father who art in Heaven, forgive us the debts of those who have violated us.

Protect children, not pedophiles.

CHAPTER FIVE

SUPPORTERS' HEALING WORK

"Think for yourself. Your minister might be wrong!"
Anonymous

INTRODUCTION

"I'm so sorry." "I'm so sorry that you were abused." "I'm so sorry that this has been so painful for you." "I know there's no way that I can take away the pain and I am with you in your recovery."

There is no script or "right thing" to say to a survivor of sexual abuse. However, there are some "wrong" things to say, or things that might trigger a response of less than appreciation from a survivor. I'm sure you can imagine the following, as well as others.

"I know exactly what you mean." "I know how you feel." "Well, you've just got to suck it up. Don't let the bastards get you down."

There are, of course, worse things to say to someone who shares that they were sexually abused by a religious or other authority. I think that you, who are reading this workbook, have heard or can imagine any number of inappropriate things to say because such comments are so much a part of our self-centered and dysfunctional culture. When you heard one of those comments, what did you do? To what degree did you understand that a response to the uncompassionate comments was needed?

I also believe that, by reading this book and learning how to be a support to survivors, you are one of the people who are more likely to be part of the solution, which is ending child abuse

everywhere, than part of the problem, which is perpetuating child abuse, actively or passively, knowingly or unknowingly, anywhere. Thank you.

A premise of therapy and support groups is that isolation maintains the deep and disabling trauma of sexual abuse. Victims often feel isolated. Victims need to have a safe environment in which they can share their stories. Your job is to be part of that safe environment, so you can listen and share your own learning.

In the first chapter, I pointed out that everyone experiences abuse of some sort in life. Many people have experienced various kinds of terrible abuse. If you have read chapters 1-4, you may now have a larger perspective about your own life hardships and a deeper connection or empathy for RASA survivors. That being said, it may be difficult to support someone else's recovery while your own processing, letting go of, or redeeming whatever kinds of abuse you have experienced is yet unfinished. While this chapter is written with those who are potential allies, resources and support people for survivors in mind, what brings you to read this workbook is the issue. This chapter is about how you take up the role of supporting victims and preventing further abuse. In a sense, it's not about you.

What I mean is that ego and expectations about what it means to be a RASA supporter or ally need to be checked at the door of actually being with survivors and dealing with lots of sad and maddening situations. The work related to your role as a RASA survivor supporter is not about your feeling better about yourself because you have done something for someone else. It's not about "you" individually. However, ending RASA is about your working with survivors in whatever way is most helpful to survivors.

This chapter will identify the key aspects of how the dynamics that sustain or promote child sexual abuse operate in groups and institutions, such as churches, temples, mosques, or other values-driven organizations. The chapter will focus on you and your role as a supporter of someone who is recovering from religious authority sexual abuse. As a supporter of a survivor, your awareness of or sensitivity to the problem of religious authority sexual abuse is necessary, although not sufficient, to be an effective ally or change agent.

THINK: WELCOME TO THE WORK

Back in the days of my K-12 administrative experience, a school in which I worked had identified "multicultural awareness" as one of the top professional development goals for the year. One teacher expressed her frustration with that goal: "I'm aware. I'm sick of being aware. Okay. Let's take that off the list." I think she felt something that is very true: awareness is not enough. I also imagine that she had the limited belief that awareness was the same as multicultural competency development. In a similar way, many survivors and supporters are very aware of the dangers of clergy sexual abuse. That, however, in no way makes us effective or authoritative religious or other sexual abuse problem solvers or survivor supporters.

Over the years, I have heard many questions regarding sexual abuse by religious authorities that have sounded naïve or cynical. I imagine that the questioners did not know very much about the experience of surviving and being transformed through clergy or other sexual abuse. The questions, nonetheless, amounted to criticizing survivors for not reporting the abuse when it was going on through questioning survivors' credibility. Some questions served to criticize survivors for reporting the abuse through interrogating the survivors' motives. After five years of excruciating scrutiny and opposition from diocesan apologists and attorneys, which in many cases exacerbated personal and professional damage to survivors, some criticized survivors for accepting a class action settlement through questioning survivors' commitment to obtaining church documents.

On the other hand, caring people may offer a caring solution that is more about them than the survivor. When I started speaking publicly about clergy sexual abuse, some outraged active Catholics arranged a "Healing Liturgy" on December 28, the Feast of the Holy Innocents. They were thoughtful in working with me to plan a liturgy that would both support survivors and engage parishioners. I wanted to see this outreach as an opportunity for many survivors to be supported, so I participated in the liturgy. Despite great publicity, only one other survivor that I knew of showed up that evening.

At one point in the liturgy, various people stood as proxies for the larger group of those who were impacted by clergy sexual abuse: disillusioned Catholics, parents and family members of sexual abuse victims, heart-broken clergy and other religious leaders, an empty chair for the church leaders and bishops, abusing clergy and religious leaders, and me, representing those who had been abused by religious authorities. Once we were all standing, others in the congregation mingled around each person and laid hands on the person and prayed in various ways for all those represented by that person. In the background, a small choir sang, "Peace is flowing like a River." I began to weep as people came by and placed a hand on me. My tears were bittersweet, as I wanted so badly to believe that these people would take the burden of speaking up and bringing about the investigations and changes that would bring the systemic abuse to the light and would make systemic changes to help victims. I also wept because it was painful for strangers to be toughing me, whether it was on my head, arm or back. I wept because the words of the song rang cold and because I felt rage, not peace, even though I wanted to be at peace with all my heart.

I believe that by keeping your role of supporting religious authority sexual abuse victims in mind, survivor supporters may better understand and transform their own betrayal, loss, or whatever impacts clergy abuse has had upon them. I hope this chapter will help you, a potential survivor supporter, walk with your brothers and sisters, who have been sexually abused by a religious authority person, through their recovery.

I also expect that anyone who claims to be an ally for victims or survivors of child sexual abuse will undergo a process of changing her mindset and way of seeing. I also expect that you will become active listeners and companions with survivors as they come to reconstruct their own identities and futures. Thank you in advance for the work that you are taking on. Welcome to the work of supporting victims of religious authority sexual abuse. Welcome to the work of ending sexual abuse. Welcome to the working pilgrimage to bring reconciliation and healing to broken individuals, groups, and organizations.

ACT 5.00: HEALING EFFORTS

How do you feel after reading about the liturgy effort described above? Please use the following list as it is or modify it to reflect upon your first reaction.

Opposed, closed, offended by survivor perspective

Ambivalent; compassionate towards survivor, yet skeptical or defensive regarding survivor perspective

Accepting of survivor perspective, along with various other feelings

Respectful of the information and perspectives of survivors and supporters

In solidarity with survivor experience, appreciative of and critical of supporters

THINK: THE PRODIGAL SON

I mentioned in chapter 1 that many psychologists consider interpersonal conflicts to be made up of ten percent present material and 90 percent past material. In chapter 2, I linked the impact of triggers, any stimulus that triggered a connection to past abuse, in survivors' contemporary experiences with unresolved past trauma. Since we all perceive and respond to information and experiences through our own filters of past experience, it is natural that your own reactions to past wrongs or perceived wrongs against yourself might impact your capacity to listen to a survivor or information about religious authority sexual or other abuse.

Consider the following statement by a survivor supporter:

> It takes time and contact with survivors to understand that mostly it's the church that left the survivors — not the other way around ... As in the story of the prodigal son, the prodigal is the Church and the Father represents the survivors. But our thinking is often entrenched in thinking WE (the church) are the center, and everyone should just 'come back to the church.'

ACT 5.01: FOLK WISDOM

Write about how the following expressions might relate to you, particularly in your understanding of and work as an advocate to support survivors and to end child sexual abuse:

Faces of others we see, but not their hearts.

One who doesn't look ahead remains behind.

Even the best cloth has an uneven thread.

One who knows nothing neither doubts nor fears anything.

The eyes believe their own evidence, the ears that of others.

One who asks a question does not err easily.

Do not be too timid nor excessively confident.

One who is ignorant at home is ignorant abroad.

The wise person never says, "I did not think."

REFLECT: WHY YOU?

In chapter 3, I discussed that with rights come responsibilities. My experience of taking responsibility for my happiness has been greatly aided by wisdom and inspiration from folks like Thich Nhat Hahn, Deepak Chopra, and others. If you are not familiar with *The Four Agreements*, by Don Miguel Ruiz, or the discussion in chapter 3, I encourage you to review the chapter. In short, they are: Let your word be impeccable; Don't take things personally; Don't assume; Do your best.

Reflect on the following questions before moving forward in the chapter:

1. To what degree does your behavior reflect the four agreements?

2. Why are you doing this (stepping forward as a survivor supporter)?

3. Why are YOU doing this? (What do you bring to this role that promotes healing and the ending of child abuse?)

THINK: WHAT ARE WE DEALING WITH?

We know more about Child Sexual Abuse (CSA) through public social services reporting than we know about the frequency of RASA, particularly as reported by religious leaders. Studies indicate that one of every four girls and one of every eight boys experience sexual abuse before the 18th birthday. We also know that only ten percent of child sexual abuse is perpetrated by strangers. Thirty percent of child sexual abuse is perpetrated by family members, and 60 percent by others known to the child. Ten percent is perpetrated by strangers; 90 percent is perpetrated by those known to the child.

Who are these perpetrators? Pedophiles span the full spectrum from saints to monsters.

Pedophiles span the full spectrum from saints to monsters. **Pedophiles span the full spectrum from saints to monsters.** In fact, over and over again pedophiles are not recognized, investigated, charged, convicted, or sent to prison simply because they are "nice guys". It is difficult enough for children and vulnerable adults to report sexual abuse at the time it is occurring, given the profound split in the psyche that takes place in children, and a profound shame in vulnerable adults. Compound the difficulty of investigating, charging and convicting pedophiles when adults do not see that these "nice people", especially religious authorities, also sexually abuse children and vulnerable adults.

ACT 5.10: PUBLIC INFORMATION

One of the most documented examinations of RASA is the Catholic church's abuse record. However, it only represents three percent of all abuse in the country. Take a few minutes to view the names and faces on these Web sites. It may come as a shock if someone you know is listed on the pages. Even if you do not know someone on the pages, know that these men and women were known to be charming, were respected, even revered, and most likely never considered to be a monster or someone capable of child rape.

http://bishop-accountability.org/member/index.jsp

http://stopbaptistpredators.org/index.htm

THINK: BELIEVING WHAT WE SEE OR SEEING WHAT WE BELIEVE

Years ago, I saw the Congressional hearings investigating the 1986 Challenger space shuttle disaster, wherein 73 seconds after liftoff seven astronauts lost their lives: Gregory Jarvis, Christie McAuliff, Ronald Mc Nair, Ellison Onizuka, Judy Resnik, Francis Scobee, and Michael Smith. The hearings revealed that there was tremendous pressure to launch the space shuttle as scheduled in order to: maintain the NASA program; further the U.S. international image as a leader in technology; enhance the Reagan administration's prestige; and extend

various aerospace industry contracts. The president even called a decision-making meeting the night of the launch and reminded the team that this was a high-stakes, high-profile project.

This context developed most notably in the year prior to this mission. During that time, in response to pressure to launch, a safety procedure shifted from proving that the launch was safe to proving that the launch was unsafe. In addition, the committee that analyzed safety conditions shrank from a group representing several stakeholders and scientists to a group of three: a member from NASA, a member from the major engineering company contracted for the mission, and an engineering supervisor.

Given the committee's predisposition to approve the Challenger space shuttle launch, one scientist, who had previously been on the launch decision-making team, came forward to appeal to the three-person board. He testified to Congress that he was so disconcerted about the proceedings that he threw photographs of the recovered fuel tanks that had been discharged in previous missions. The pictures showed deterioration of the O-rings that sealed the fuel from the shuttle.

He pointed out that there was something wrong and dangerous with the O-rings and that he thought the temperature of the launch was significant. In other words, the colder the temperature of the launch conditions, the more the O-rings deteriorated. He reported that he had shouted at the board that previous missions had been dangerous and that they needed to reconsider a decision to launch. The response he got from the committee was that he did not have enough evidence to support his claims. The committee decided to launch.

This story illustrates how very smart and experienced people can be blind to new information that contradicts what they want or believe. In this case, the "evidence" that the board member was asking for was what is known as traditional, quantitative research. This is the result of interpreting a data set of hundreds or thousands of examples taken and measured under particular conditions. This kind of evidence may take years to accumulate and interpret, using mathematical correlations. Even though there was physical evidence and there was witness and experience of someone closest to the launches, the board members couldn't believe what they saw. Instead they could only see what they believed was scientific evidence.

ACT 5.11: DEALING WITH DISASTER

What parallels do you recognize in this disaster and in the religious authority sexual abuse disaster?

How would you describe yourself in terms of being an ally or advocate for those who have been sexually abused by religious authorities or others?

     1   **2**   **3**   **4**   **5**

What descriptors do you ascribe to each of the numbers, 1-5, regarding being an ally or advocate for those who have been sexually abused by religious authorities or others?

Give an example that serves as evidence of your self-assessment. What was the outcome?

Sexual abuse is sexual contact without the full and free consent of both people. Any time there is a power imbalance, one person has less opportunity and inclination to say no. Sexual contact between an adult and child, or minister and follower, is clearly across a difference in power and is absolutely wrong.

A survivor describes how a priest got him drunk and took his bathing suit off. He knew something was wrong, but his mother had always told him to obey priests. "I really didn't feel that I ought to trust him. But I didn't dare contradict him. And he said, 'All I'm doing is, I want to check you out; I just want to see if you're healthy.' It went on for three years until the priest found someone else."

A recent argument by church bishops to be excused for culpability in managing religious authorities who sexually abuse children is instructive regarding the difficulty of investigating, charging and prosecuting pedophiles. The November, 2007, John Jay study intimates that "Sex abuse in the Roman Catholic Church mirrors Society as a whole." In response, Andrew Greeley writes,

> The team searching for an explanation of pederasty gave a verbal preview of their findings to be reported in full later in the year. The cause of the problem seems to be change in sexual morals and media imagery. The bishops will love that and so will the Vatican -- a cause of the problem that is external to the Church. Blame the people for their sexual mores and the media for their exploitation of the human body, not why so many bishops denied the problem for so long.

Perhaps some pedophiles have been removed from employment in an organization or have been incarcerated. Perhaps you have shared in the efforts to punish pedophiles, with outrage, or support victims in your organization, with compassion. To date, only two percent of priests who are known or credibly accused to be child molesters have spent even one day in prison for this criminal behavior. The truth is that religious authority sexual abuse is more than a collection of individual, pathological behaviors. Given the evidence, we need to reconsider child sexual abuse as a systemic problem and ourselves as an essential part in the system.

In 2002, the U.S. Conference of Catholic Bishops responded to allegations of widespread child abuse and cover-up by priests by commissioning a study with the John Jay College of Criminal Justice. In February, 2004, the report on the years between 1950 and 2002, based upon church records, revealed:

Eleven thousand allegations of sexual abuse of children by priests: 6,700 (61%) substantiated; 1,000 (9.1%) unsubstantiated. Three thousand, three-hundred cases were not investigated because the allegations were made after the priest's death. The report went on to summarize factors that contributed to clergy sexual abuse:

- Failure by the hierarchy to grasp the seriousness of the problem.
- Overemphasis on the need to avoid a scandal.
- Use of unqualified treatment centers.
- Misguided willingness to forgive.
- Insufficient accountability.

Another aspect of religious authority sexual abuse is the way that religious authorities work to promote truth and reconciliation. According to the OC Weekly, we will never know the full scope of the abuse because many dioceses destroyed or withheld personnel files. Much attention has been given to the 508 individual cases in L.A., the 144 survivors of clergy molestation in San Diego, and 90 survivors in diocese of Orange. At this writing, nearly a year after the alleged settlements by diocesan leaders to halt the public trials of clergy abuse, renewed efforts to block the release of abuser files are in the news.

By conservative estimates, the numbers of cases that are currently known represent ten percent of the actual instances of abuse by these same abusers. It is troubling that these religious authorities worked within social systems that effectively assisted them in taking advantage of children and vulnerable adults. Even more troubling is the conclusion that there are many people who knew or should have known that children and vulnerable adults were or are being sexually abused.

ACT 5.12: WHAT MUST I DO?

The following are some implications that one survivor supporter has identified for herself with respect to systemic understanding and transformation. Which statements are part of your current actions? Which are next steps for you to take as a survivor supporter?

- I must do more than trust the bishops to make policy changes.
- I must actively support survivors by my presence, and actions.
- I must educate Catholics about the experiences of clergy abuse survivors by speaking up.
- I must be willing to be uncomfortable and allow others to feel uncomfortable when faced with new, possibly unwelcome information about CSA.
- Mostly I must act like an adult—and expect others to be adults when areas that need change become obvious to me, or when policies are not adequate, or when policies are not followed.

What other actions which are particular to your role or responsibilities in your church or values-driven organization can you add to your list?

THINK: PARALLELS TO PRIVILEGE AND RACISM

Beverly Daniel Tatum offers a very useful and parallel discussion of racism, not as individual acts, but as a system of hidden conditions that privilege some and work against others. She offers the image of a moving sidewalk at an airport as a way to respond to the person who claims, "I'm not racist", yet who does not actively work to end racism. Borrowing her image to frame how religious authority child sexual abuse has persisted, consider that a very small percentage of people are pedophiles.

Whenever people find out about Religious Authority Sexual Abuse, it is common to hear about their outrage, disgust, or disbelief. Recall many national tragedies, whether they are school shootings, corporate pillaging a la Enron, a natural disaster like Hurricane Katrina, or the national and international unfolding of religious authority child sexual abuse. Emotional or visceral responses to human suffering may be necessary, but in themselves are not sufficient to transform cultural or institutional conditions that allow RASA. An emotional response may be more of an ego-centric response than something that is helpful to RASA victims or survivors. An intellectual response may be more of an "ethno-centric" response, reflecting a set of beliefs that shape what we interpret or understand. Action based upon learning from the conditions that allowed for tragedies is what will prevent Religious Authority Sexual Abuse.

No one may claim to be an advocate or to be anti-abuse, likewise, without taking action to support victims, and prevent future abuse. No one may claim to be an advocate or to be anti-abuse without taking action to transform the hidden system and overt behaviors that lead to RASA. The moving sidewalk that leads to RASA is in place. In other words, we don't have to "do anything" to contribute to the system or operation of overt behaviors that lead to child sexual abuse. We contribute by going along and standing still. Adults cannot claim to be innocent or neutral in this discussion.

Tatum's argument brings up the context in which we all live and in which some have been sexually abused. Part of a context is seen in the shared, visible aspects of a culture or group. The part of the context that I want to highlight here is internal: the "warm feelings" about the church and the way it can be a good part of a person's life at every phase. For some people, that good feeling is ripped from them, and they lose their comfortable connection in the church family—they lose their holidays, the rhythms and routines, the place to celebrate milestone moments, etc. On the other hand, many faithful churchgoers can only consider the damage related to RASA as relating to priests who are tainted by the scandal, or by low morale. As one veteran survivor supporter noted, "[this] is a typical mind set that is hard to change in a view of church. The person is not being deliberately defensive — she just doesn't see a different point of view yet." The fact that a person doesn't recognize the damage related to RASA in a group or organization doesn't mean it is not there. An adult cannot claim to be a survivor supporter without taking action to support victims of RASA and working to end RASA.

ACT 5.13: WHAT DOES IT MEAN TO BE AN ADVOCATE?

What does it mean to you to be an advocate or to be anti-abuse?

What do you understand by the statement that we don't have to "do anything" to contribute to the system or operation in place?

How would you respond to a survivor who said that the average churchgoer acts as if emotion and religious feeling equal change or the righting of wrongs?

Although you may not have been sexually abused by a religious authority, I believe you have been impacted by that abuse. Whether you practice atheism, humanism, or have been a faithful, contributing member of a particular church, you may have experienced the meaning of the strange admonition, "Pray to be disillusioned." I was given that advice many years ago by an ex-superintendent who was speaking to a group of idealistic future school administrators. At the time, I thought the advice-giver was merely cynical, remembering the adage that cynics are idealists who have been hurt.

As a teacher, researcher, and teacher educator, however, I have seen the impact of "seeing others, not as they are, but as we are". I have experienced how intelligent people, like some prominent scientists, can see what they believe they are looking for rather than believe what they see. I have seen how good people also hold on to some illusions that serve them in some way, but which can lead them to compound the isolation, mistrust, and rage that victims of religious authority sexual abuse too often experience. This is what I referred to earlier in the chapter about how past experiences or beliefs can interfere with how we take in new information about RASA.

As you have come to learn about the breadth and depth of RASA, I imagine that the ways you consider yourself to be a defender of the faith may have changed. I know many active survivor supporters who have come to understand how they have been misled or allowed themselves to be misled by religious authorities. In effect, non-abused survivor supporters have experienced some of the betrayal that victims of religious authority sexual abuse have experienced, but from a different perspective. This is the point at which that strange admonition can be useful. Once disillusioned, you are now in a position to step back and examine how you have previously understood your role or what role, knowingly or unknowingly, you may have played and make a conscious decision about what role you will now play: cheerleader, bystander, or ally.

Another way of thinking of these terms is to review the workbook introduction. In short, some non-abused survivor supporters will move from unconsciously incompetent (cheerleaders) to consciously incompetent (oblivious bystanders); from consciously incompetent (guilty bystanders) to consciously competent (allies); from consciously competent (allies) to unconsciously competent (change agents). The process may be very challenging as non-abused survivor supporters move between levels of understanding or consciousness: from "blind roles" to "hidden roles"; from hidden roles to private roles; from private roles to public roles. The process of reconciling new experiences with our prior understandings offers non-abused survivor supporters an opportunity to move forward into a deeper capacity to understand the complex problems and solutions related to RASA.

ACT 5.20: THE BENEFITS OF DISILLUSIONMENT

How have you been disillusioned, in general, that has led to growth or an increase in effectiveness?

Given your example, which change in consciousness does it relate to:

A move from being unconsciously incompetent to consciously incompetent? How?

A move from being consciously incompetent to consciously competent? How?

A move from being consciously competent to unconsciously competent? How?

Where in the continuum might you be regarding being a survivor supporter? What evidence can you identify to support your self-assessment?

THINK: CHEERLEADERS

I've never been a cheerleader, but I have been a fan or fanatic when my kids participated in school sports. Cheerleaders are like super-fans. They publicly support or foster belief in someone or in a group despite evidence to the contrary. Cheerleaders amplify strengths and minimize faults. With respect to religious authority sexual abusers, I apply the term to those people, or even policies that are supported by individuals, who seem to be blind to abuse and its dynamics, and instead defend an abuser, group, or institution as if past or present abuse weren't true.

In the following section, I've borrowed language for a partner of a Child Sexual Abuse (CSA) perpetrator or parent of the sexually abused child. I believe that you can translate the language: home = parish; parent or partner = parishioner— to relate to parishes or churches. Cheerleaders in either scenario excuse, ignore, or allow the following behaviors when allegations of sexual abuse arise:

- Perpetrator continues to live in the home after disclosure

- Perpetrator continues to visit the home daily, assuming children are out of the home
- Parent or partner appears to have no other support system
- Parent or partner does many errands for or takes care of business for perpetrator
- Parent or partner has virtually no interests that do not involve perpetrator
- Parent or partner talks daily to perpetrator on the phone
- Parent or partner is not able to express any negative feelings toward perpetrator; says everything is alright
- Parent or partner regularly expresses concern for perpetrator's welfare, rarely referring to victim's welfare.

CSA cheerleader language might sound like the following statements which imply that the victim is to blame or is not credible:

- "She has always been seductive or sexy. She or he seduced him."
- "He couldn't control himself when she or

he came onto him." "It was those clothes she wore, or the alcohol or stress."

Cheerleader language also might imply that another group or system is to blame for the group's problems:

- "We were fine till attorneys came into the picture, SNAP got involved, the psychologist gave bad advice", etc.

ACT 5.21: CHEERLEADERS

How do these behaviors relate to your parish, church or organization?

What relates to you or your environment?

If not to you, how do the statements relate to others in your environment?

What do you think is the next step for you in order to be an ally?

THINK: OBLIVIOUS BYSTANDERS

"You stay out of my business and I'll stay out of yours." That's the code of ethics I think relates to being a bystander. That might work in highly individualistic settings where group members have no sense of responsibility to one another. This belief may be part of what happened in the infamous Kitty Genovese murder. In this case many people witnessed a brutal and protracted murder, but did not intervene based on the assumption that someone else would take action.

The Genovese case may be extreme, yet it relates to RASA in that some may be oblivious to what is going on while others can be stuck in inaction. These are whom I consider oblivious bystanders. They may believe that some

individuals or even policies may address abuse in principle. In other words, abuse may be happening in other organizations, but not their own. By "guilty bystander", I mean individuals that recognize abuse and purport to intend to end abuse, but who do not act to challenge, interrupt or change abusive practices, environments or systems.

Oblivious bystanders are parents or members of religious or other organizations who do not see or act on such warning signs related to CSA. For example, parents should beware of anyone who wants to be with their children more than they do. Everyone should be aware that preferential child molesters seduce children much the same way adults seduce one another. Oblivious bystanders:

- regularly allow children to be baby-sat or supervised by people who demonstrate "red-flag" behaviors, such as active alcoholics or grandparents who have a history of abuse;
- allow children to be baby-sat or supervised by people unknown or little known to family or parent;
- have been told by child or others about molest behaviors, but continue to allow contact between molester and child.

There are many reasons parents and others take up a role of oblivious bystander; I believe that a major one is ambivalence. In the literal, root sense of the term, *ambi-valent*, there are two values coexisting in the bystander that may lead to conflict or confusion: belief and experience; loyalty and responsibility, etc.

When allegations of RASA arise, oblivious bystanders may:

- vacillate between believing and not believing, for example by keeping up contact and relationship with perpetrator;
- vacillate between blaming the perpetrator or him or herself and blaming the victim.
- believe misinformation that the church "has no choice" but to file for bankruptcy, that the church is victimized by survivors

In the case of the parent of the child being abused, the bystander parent may have a support system of family, friends or therapist to talk to, but does not talk about or acknowledge sexual abuse as an area of concern.

Oblivious bystanders' language may sound like:

- "I found out that a priest was molesting the school girls, including two daughters of my closest friends. I had no idea."

ACT 5.22: OBLIVIOUS BYSTANDERS

How do these behaviors relate to your parish or church?

What relates to you or your environment?

If not to you, how do the statements relate to others in your environment?

What is the next step for you to take in order to be an ally?

THINK: GUILTY BYSTANDERS

Unlike an oblivious bystander, who may embody the description of someone who does not know what he or she knows (DK K), a guilty bystander knows that something is wrong that may involve sexual abuse. Such behavior may look like:

- Reporting concerns to friends or relatives, but not reporting to authorities.

- Understanding the value of screening supervisors and babysitters, but, when under stress, appears to give up authority and control to anyone who will help her or him out of a bind.

Guilty bystander language may sound like the following statements which imply that the perpetrator is responsible or that the parent recognizes her own failure to protect the child. The parent may express anger, fear, or anxiety, but it is not aimed at victim:

- "He or she should have known better." "How could he have done this to us?" "After all this time, I thought I knew him."

- "I should have known." "I am angry with myself for not picking up on the clues."

ACT 5.23: GUILTY BYSTANDERS

How do these behaviors relate to your parish or church?

What relates to you or your environment?

If not to you, how do the statements relate to others in your environment?

What is the next step for you to take in order to be an ally?

THINK: SOME OF WHAT DO WE KNOW ABOUT ABUSERS

Ten years after the 1996 murder of JonBenet Ramsey, a writer for The New York Times lurked online at pedophile chat rooms, and wrote about the chilling way pedophiles convince themselves that children want to have sex with them and insinuate themselves into the lives of children. In a bigger social picture, JonBenet Ramsey's death and the whole circus surrounding it even ten years later have

everything to do with the culture's inclination to sexualize children.

Sex trafficking, involving children and women, is a local and global problem. It is listed along with drug trafficking, money laundering, high-tech crime and environmental crime as threats to the United States and the world. In my region of the world, I have even seen a large sign in English for visitors from the U.S. goint into Tijuana that reads, "Child prostitution is a crime." The question must be asked and answered, "Who is this for?"

Recall that these perpetrators span the full spectrum from saints to monsters. In spite of this fact, over and over again pedophiles are not recognized, investigated, charged, convicted, or sent to prison simply because they are "nice guys". Some pedophiles are preferential offenders. Some of these pedophiles are situational offenders. Finally, some are "indiscriminant or sadistic" offenders.

All of them use the existing social or organizational system of trust, access, and authorization that is in place to sexually abuse children and vulnerable adults. Although a variety of individuals sexually abuse children, preferential-type sex offenders, and especially pedophiles, are the primary acquaintance sexual exploiters of children. In Tatum's discussion, this small percentage of people would be comparable to active racists within a context in which racism is barely acknowledged or understood.

Because there is limited research about religious authorities who are arrested and jailed for child sexual abuse, I borrow from something we know more about in order to illustrate a point for survivor supporters: domestic violence. The following statements are adapted from Paul Kivel's *Men's Work: How to Stop the Violence that Tears our Lives Apart*, related to male violence upon children, wives or partners.

> The present is not simply the result of all past experiences and training. Not everyone who is sexually assaulted commits sexual assault. Not every boy who is beaten up grows up to beat his children, wife, or partner. Men decide to commit acts of violence. Men decide whether to take responsibility for those acts or to avoid responsibility. There are standard tactics men who are abusive use to avoid responsibility.

> Denial: "I didn't hit her." If the denial doesn't hold up because of the evidence, for example, she has a broken arm, bruises, or miscarriage, then the violence is minimized. "I didn't hit her. Well, it was only a slap."

> When the minimization doesn't hold up because she is in the hospital, then the batterer's justification shifts to a combination of justifying the violence and blaming the victim. "She asked for it." Or, "She should have known not to say that to me."

Kivel goes on to describe other responses to victims or to those who support the victims:

> **Redefinition:** "It was mutual combat. She hit me first. It takes two to fight."
> **Intentionality:** "I didn't intend to hit her. I didn't mean to hit her so hard. Things got out of hand. I didn't mean to …"
> **Distance present from past:** "It's all over with. I'll never do it again."
> **Infrequency:** "It was an isolated incident."
> **Counterattack with competing victimization:** "She's really the one who has all the power over me."

ACT 5.24: RESPONSES YOU HAVE HEARD

Think of the responses that you have heard or said about victims who come forward and have accused a priest or other religious authority of sexual abuse. How do these responses relate to the descriptions or statements above?

How do the statements you have in mind relate to the categories of: abuser, cheerleader, bystander, or ally?

THINK: ALLIES

The expression, "I know that someone discovered water, but I don't think it was a fish" comes to mind when I think of RASA allies. In order for someone to take action to protect victims of sexual abuse, he or she must have enough perspective, health, and consciousness to intervene in an abusive situation. Somehow, allies bring an experience or perspective outside of the environment in which cheerleaders and bystanders find comfort and unquestioning loyalty.

Allies do not need to be family members. Allies do not need to be perfect. The following descriptions use the language for a partner of a child sexual abuse perpetrator or parent of the sexually abused child. Translate the language to relate to parishes or churches.

Ally behaviors look like:

- Parent has asked perpetrator to leave environment and she or he has not returned.

- Parent does not have regular, constant visitation with perpetrator
- Parent allows perpetrator to care for his own needs; cares for his or her needs and those of the children.
- Parent has support system of family, friends, etc.
- Parent has own interests and life independent of perpetrators
- Parent expresses ambivalence about reunification; maintains a "wait and see" attitude.

Ally statements sound like the parent or ally believes the child (no ambivalence)

- "She would not lie about something like this."
- "I raised her to tell the truth and I believe she would not lie."

Parent expresses to perpetrator her anger and other negative feelings toward perpetrator.

ACT 5.25: ALLIES

How do these behaviors relate to your parish or church?

What relates to you or your environment?

If not to you, how do the statements relate to others in your environment?

What is the next step for you to take in order to be an ally?

THINK: RISKS OF ACTING AS AN ALLY

Anyone may sometimes be the recipient of survivors' critique or anger, even allies. Imagine the following scenario. Perhaps it is in a listening session, wherein someone, but not a survivor, laments the fact that so many good priests are being tainted by the bad behavior of a few pedophiles or uncooperative bishops. A survivor responds angrily:

"Hmm, tainted or raped? Tainted or thrown into a state, if not a life, of disassociation with our bodies, minds, and hearts? Tainted or spiritually razed? I'll take tainted. I'm not a fan of blaming folks for what they didn't do. In this case, however, I know that lots of survivors are furious that priests and others saw suspicious behavior, like kids sleeping in the same bed, excessively affectionate kisses, touches, gifts and special attention being given to some kids, etc., if not

undeniable evidence of sexual abuse—and they didn't do anything. Didn't call CPS. Didn't talk to the kid involved and ask questions. Didn't interrupt or chaperone or question. Didn't pull the abuser aside and confront or express some concern after acknowledging whatever feelings of confusion, outrage, fear or other myriad of human responses to such an experience.

Or what they did amounted to nothing, as the victim never knew, the parents never knew, other grown-ups never knew and the behavior continued. In my mind we're all tainted by our inaction and someone who defends priests, who took no action to protect kids from sexual abuse, is defending herself more than another grown-up who needs to be able to withstand the challenges and critiques of someone living the gospel, for being prophetic, not pathetic!"

ACT 5.26: PROPHETIC, NOT PATHETIC

What thoughts come to you about the survivor's words?

What feelings come to you about the survivor's angry tone?

What would you do or say in this setting, either immediately or later?

How do you assess your responses (cheerleader, oblivious bystander, guilty bystander, ally)? What evidence can you point to of having behaved in these ways in other situations?

THINK: LOOKS LIKE, SOUNDS LIKE, FEELS LIKE

Think of a church or organization that you are familiar with, in which a known or alleged child sexual abuser has been or is currently a member. Here are some examples of what being a cheerleader, oblivious bystander, guilty bystander, and advocate might look like, sound like, and feel like in that church or organization.

	Action logic	Looks like	Sounds like	Feels like
Cheerleader	Individuals or policies seem to be **Blind** to essential knowledge	Eyes closed. Jaws clenched	"Catholic bashing"; "Priests are only human"	Defensiveness, fear and anger.
Ignorant Bystander	Essential knowledge is **Hidden**, yet recognizable in other organizations	Paralyzed inaction;	"We shouldn't focus on the church, when this problem is more prevalent in other parts of society."	May feel the need to keep further information at bay in order NOT to challenge their world view.
Guilty bystander	Essential knowledge is available or accessible to a select few or as an organizational **Private knowledge**	Leaves it to others; Will "leave it to God" to judge."	"We don't know the whole story and shouldn't judge."	Comfortable with obedience, and uncomfortable with adult thinking.
Ally	Essential knowledge is useful and made **Public**	Openly supports and advocates for victims.	"Where is the open disclosure, education and accountability inside and outside the church?"	Feels betrayed, angry, sad, but ready for action to create an open climate within the church where abuse will be recognized and reported

ACT 5.27: LOOKS LIKE, SOUNDS LIKE, FEELS LIKE

What similarities do you see in your own church or organization?

What similarities do you share with others you have described in the exercise above?

	Action logic	Looks like	Sounds like	Feels like
You				
Other(s)				

What do you now know, think, or feel as a result of this comparison?

What will you now do differently as a result of your insight?

THINK: HOW IS CHILD SEXUAL ABUSE PERCEIVED AND PERPETUATED?

In Kivel's work, he reports that the deterrent that keeps most men from continuing to hit their partners is arrest, the use of the criminal justice system. However, this deals with the symptoms and not the problems underlying the behavior. Similarly, the removal of individual abusers from an organization does not address the problems underlying the behavior.

The film "Little Children" illustrates the dynamic that when adults do not manage their own boundaries, it is difficult for them to manage other boundaries to protect children from sexual abuse. Subsequently, some grooming or testing behaviors that may take place right in front of their eyes may be missed, even though they may seem obvious in retrospect.

CSA GROOMING BEHAVIORS

I have already mentioned that parents should beware of anyone who wants to be with their children more than they do. Preferential child molesters seduce children much the same way adults seduce one another. A primary

difference, however, is that these grooming or testing behaviors take place when a parent or caretaker gives a child molester access to and a kind of authority over the child. The following are some of the grooming or testing behaviors that perpetrators use to establish physical, emotional, and intellectual dominance or control over their victims:

- Treating child different from other kids
- Wanting to spend time alone with child, making excuses to go places or have others leave
- Doing things to child or asking her to do things that involve physical contact, like giving backrubs, washing perpetrator's back, tickling, messaging her or wanting to help child wash
- Accidentally —on purpose— touching victim's private parts, brushing against breasts while wrestling, rubbing body against child, etc.
- Looking at or touching child's body and saying it is an inspection or to see how child is developing
- Putting lotion or ointment on when parent or others are not around or when nothing is wrong
- Accidentally —on purpose— coming into child's room without knocking, not allowing child to close doors to bedroom or bathroom
- Asking questions or making accusations about sexual issues between child and boyfriend or girlfriend
- Teaching sex education by showing pornographic pictures, showing her or his body or touching child
- Saying sexual things about child's body or how victim dresses
- Talking to child about sexual things he or she has done
- Saying to child that he or she is special, different, the only one who really understands
- Giving child special privileges or favors and making child feel obligated
- Treating child meaner than others
- Not letting child have friends or do things that other kids of same age do
- Telling child not to tell parent or other people about things that happen between child and perpetrator
- Coming into bedroom at night
- Accidentally —on purpose— letting robe come apart, walking without clothes on

Child sexual abuse as a systemic problem means that each person in the group or organization in which CSA takes place is part of the problem and solution, not either-or. When adults observe or hear about any of the abovementioned behaviors taking place, they might act according to the roles.

ACT 5.28: WHAT DOES IT MEAN TO YOU?

What does it mean to you to take up a role in an organization or system in which you wish to end or prevent religious authority sexual abuse? Use the chart to analyze responses and behaviors you have noticed in the past or have recently become aware of.

Perpetrator Behavior	Role	Response may look like	Response may sound like	Response may feel like
	Cheerleader			
	Ignorant Bystander			
	Guilty bystander			

Perpetrator Behavior	Role	Response may look like	Response may sound like	Response may feel like
	Ally			
	Other			

In chapter 1, I identified several warning signs, such as sudden changes in behavior that victims of CSA manifest. Consider responses to these behaviors through the lenses of the roles already identified:

- Stealing from others, whether it be material or emotional;
- Addictive lifestyles (self or other destructive lifestyles);
- Anti-social behavior that seems like competitiveness or aggressiveness;
- Physical aggression or bullying (abusing others' minds, hearts, or bodies);
- Pseudomature behavior;
- Persistent and inappropriate sexual play with peers or toys or with themselves, or sexually aggressive behavior with others.

To someone taking up a role of "cheerleader" or "oblivious bystander", I imagine that such sudden change of behavior might not be seen as more than as an "individual" problem or change in personality or style. I believe this same lens may be a liability for those same people. I received a note from an ex-priest that I believe illustrates the idea that some who have taken up a role of "cheerleader" or "bystander" before learning about religious authority sexual abuse have later become "casualties" of a closed system that perpetuated RASA.

"I am very pleased you and others like you are standing up for this. About two years ago, I found out that a priest with whom I shared St. _____ rectory in San Diego, and his brother, a retired Irish diocesan priest, who lived across the street, were molesting the school girls, including two daughters of my closest friends. The offending priests are both dead and their karma is being worked out in another sphere. What astonishes me is that the pastor and I had no inkling this was going on and that no one spoke out even though, as it apparently turns out, it was even known by some adults in the parish. What sickens me is that they could get up in front of a congregation, celebrate the Eucharist, and preach, preach very moralistically indeed. ….

Yes, I did leave the priesthood and ultimately the Roman Church for various reasons but it was a happy divorce. I needed to move on, move on especially when more and more I knew I could not teach what was required of me because I simply no longer believed it."

I believe that those who rely on individual compassion or outrage as a response to RASA also may become casualties in the unfolding tragedy.

ACT 5.29: RESPONSES

If you haven't seen the film "Doubt", rent it. List the various signs of sexual abuse throughout the film.

List the various roles taken up by the adults.

REFLECT: DEEP LEARNING

In chapter 3, I noted the difficult learning process for survivors to let go of older models or ways of thinking and problem-solving in order to be more effective, intentional and purposeful. "Survivor-thrivers enter into new psychological ground with respect to reconstructing our self-understanding, self-acceptance and self-development. This comes as a result of moving beyond the raw, reactive experiences of survivorhood and being willing to Not Know what we Don't Know (DK DK)."

I imagine that this new information, when applied to your particular context and experience, may also be difficult. I believe that supporters face a similar challenge in moving forward: "Survivor-thrivers shift from living as surviving to living as choosing, willing to move forward through anxiety, frustration and disequilibrium into a deeper level of complexity and capacity to understand any problem and any solution in more and more ways."

Einstein said, "No problem can be solved from the same consciousness that created it. We must learn to see the world anew." Consider that all of your past experiences have led you to be here now, reading this material and re-thinking your role as an ally, contemplating in action. Thank you for responding to your call to support survivors and to change practices that led to abuse.

WHAT ARE SOME IMPLICATIONS FOR ALLIES OF **RASA** VICTIMS?

THINK: INDIVIDUAL HEALTHY RESPONSES TO RELIGIOUS AUTHORITY SEXUAL ABUSE

At the beginning of this chapter, I said, "victims need to have a safe environment in which they can share their stories. Your job is to be part of that safe environment, so you can listen and share your own learning." The following is not an exhaustive list of healthy responses to religious authority sexual abuse, and it is a good beginning.

Victim:
- Can talk about the molest
- Can talk about feelings about the molest
- Each family member has had appropriate therapy: individual, family, couples, group, etc.
- There are no family secrets: each family member is aware of the molest, alcoholism, etc. Ideally, this includes extended family members, kinship support people.
- Other serious issues are resolved: non-protective parents' drug problem, perpetrators' battering etc.
- Family therapy has taken place
- Therapists for the minor and family concur
- There is no denial of the molest by family and household members
- The victim feels safe with the perpetrator in the home.

Non-protecting parent or adults in organization
- Recognizes and verbalizes that molest of the child did happen
- Is not doing so in an ambivalent way: "I believe her and I believe him."
- Knows perpetrator did it, knows what happened and is not minimizing
- Recognizes own issues, role he or she played, history of organization issues, etc.
- Has had recommended therapy or treatment for those issues and the current molest problem
- This parent has resolved other issues: mental health problems, drug use, etc.
- This parent has worked on couples, marital, sibling, conjoint therapy or other recommended components of the plan and any parent-child problems.
- Family therapy has taken place and the therapists involved in the case agree the non-protecting parent can protect.

Perpetrator
- Acknowledges the molest of victim
- Recognizes the role he or she played in the molest and takes responsibility for the molest.
- Has worked on perpetrator role and actions of molest in therapy by an approved therapist.
- Has assimilated, progressed, internalized, shown progress in resolving those issues in therapy
- Has provided the victim with an atonement statement for the molest, a written or verbal statement, or both, acknowledging what happened, that she or he regrets it and that it will not happen again
- Has done the same for the partner if re-unification will take place with the partner
- Has demonstrated that she or he has progressed in empathy, power and control methods of coping, maturity level, etc.
- Has resolved other issues, such as alcoholism, domestic violence, etc., and progressed in components of her or his plan.
- Therapists for father and family concur that it is safe
- Family therapy has taken place

Siblings and members of organization
- Are aware of the molest, understand what happened

- Have progressed or resolved issues regarding self, other family members in therapy regarding the molest

- Have worked on or resolved any other issues, such as anger or out of control behaviors in therapy

ACT 5.30: ASSESSING ORGANIZATIONAL SUB-GROUPS

Take time to review the previous lists and assign a point value to how well the following statements relate to people with whom you are working. After adding up the total points, share your results and insight with colleague.

1) not at all/very little   3) sometimes/somewhat   5) often/very much

What similarities do you share with others you have described in the exercise above?

What do you now know, think, or feel as a result of this comparison?

What will you now do differently as a result of your insight?

THINK: COLLECTIVE LEARNING PROCESS—PHASE 1

The working assumption in this workbook is that we all need to bring our critical thinking skills or questioning skills to bear upon previously unquestioned or unnoticed areas in order to prevent and end child sexual abuse. A corollary assumption is that **this work is profoundly difficult**. The experience and temporary consequence of this difficult learning is often marked by anxiety, frustration, and disequilibrium.

There are many times when an uncomfortable sense of "not knowing" may take place, albeit as a result of markedly distinctive levels of understanding. Just as individuals experience deep learning, groups and institutions may develop a collective culture of deep learning. Regarding responding to allegations of religious authority sexual abuse, there is an identifiable process of

conversion that takes place. It occurs roughly in four phases: initial denial, attempts at containment, commitment to justice, victims' advocacy.

In Phase I, Church officials have difficulty believing victims' allegations. Sometimes this takes the form of a complete denial. For example, despite allegation after allegation against the same person, religious leaders may steadfastly refuse to believe the charges. A more common form of denial is an often-heard remark about victims, "They're just in it for the money." This is said despite the fact that the majority of victims do not ask for monetary damages.

Frequently, the denial takes the form of a minimization. Some will minimize the responsibility of the perpetrator by blaming the victim. For example, they might say, "The victim was coming on to the minister."

Another form of minimization is emphasizing the reality of false allegations. While recovered memories are less credible than a memory of abuse that was never repressed, religious authorities have too often dismissed the reality of child sexual abuse as a phenomenon promoted by irresponsible therapists and their clients' false memories. The reality is that the vast majority of allegations of child sexual abuse are true.

Similarly, a third form of minimization is not perceiving the widespread nature of sexual misconduct and its potentially devastating effects. While admitting that sexual abuse sometimes happens, Church hierarchies have sometimes downplayed the importance of the issue and how serious its implications are.

Treating the issue of sexual misconduct as a minor issue that needs passing attention by religious authorities is a type of minimization. Denial and minimization by religious authorities re-victimizes those who have been harmed by clerical sexual misconduct. It also obstructs the healing of the Church.

Phase I may look like:
- No documents available to public;
- Obstructionist behavior to release information;
- Denial of problem, even in the face of evidence;
- Millions of dollars spent on public relations and attorney fees;
- Documents or letters that confirm cover up, child endangerment; gaps in documentation;
- Air and water, or bishops and religious authorities live in separate worlds and operate by different rules than the rest of society

Phase I may sound like:
- Concern for privacy of pedophiles far outweighs rights of public or concern for abused; bishop-priest confidentiality, or other references to lega or bureaucratic justification; Prisoner or Victim complaints, wherein clergy or "faithful" take no significant responsibility for abuse;
- Blaming others for church bashing;
- Blaming victims and victim advocates as liars or money chasers.

ACT 5.31: COLLECTIVE LEARNING PROCESS – PHASE 1

What have you seen or heard from religious leaders and members relative to Phase 1?

How did you respond?

What was the outcome of your action?

THINK: COLLECTIVE LEARNING PROCESS—PHASE 2

Once the initial denial has been overcome and religious authorities begin to recognize the prevalence and destructiveness of clerical sexual misconduct, they often move into Phase II. Here, the approach is to limit the public and financial exposure of the Church. Attempts at containment in Phase II are a minimalistic approach driven by legal and public relations concerns.

Faced with a potentially disastrous situation, religious leaders will then seek to contain the problem, that is, deal with it as quietly and expeditiously as possible. Churches are becoming aware of how damaging public revelations of such misconduct are. They are acutely aware of how financially costly civil suits can be. In Phase II, they may try to distance themselves from the perpetrator and his or her actions. Religious leaders once attempted containment in the form of settling civil suits with a "gag" order for the victim, insisting the victim not speak of the abuse publicly. In this phase, religious leaders rarely, if ever, speak about the issue of sexual misconduct publicly. If they do, it is in the face of intense media pressure due to a highly public case of abuse. Even then, their comments are only to assure their congregations that they have the situation well in hand.

Phase II may look like:
- Posting statements and limited information about abusers or public safety responses on Web sites, after being mandated by court or not in accessible areas;
- Beginning "safe church" training programs, but not in concert with survivors;
- Religious leaders' and defenders' seeking most convenient method of realizing short-term change or reduction of symptom with little group educational process;
- Oil and Vinegar, or Bishops and supporters are different and float above the rest of society or "faithful".

Phase II may sound like:
- William Donahue, president of Catholic League on MSNBC blasting Robin Williams' comedy references to clergy child sexual abuse as "Catholic bashing";
- Donahue and others arguing that any reporting that is critical of bishop and parishioner collusion or cover up behavior regarding clergy sexual abuse is a double standard compared to Don Imus or others who have publicly insulted groups;
- Talking without having listened to survivors or having read the literature and real documentation of clergy abuse;
- Religious Tourists and Consumers — believing superficial experiences and others' reports that validate their beliefs about others, victims and their supporters;
- Church apologists and defenders placing onus of responsibility on a program or person without changing behavior that led to abuse;
- Defensive comments that divert attention from the problem; for example, "What about teachers, other churches?"; "but he's such a good man—how is it possible?"

ACT 5.32: COLLECTIVE LEARNING PROCESS – PHASE 2

What have you seen or heard from religious leaders and members relative to Phase II?

How did you respond?

What was the outcome of your action?

THINK: COLLECTIVE LEARNING PROCESS-- PHASE 3

Phase III still appears to be more theoretical than real, regarding a heart-felt commitment to the healing of victims, perpetrators and the wider Church. Conventional wisdom seems to be that this conversion to Phase III takes place when a church leader actually sits down with victims of clerical sexual misconduct and truly listens. While there have been many powerful moments between victims and leaders, this is far from a true dialogue.

Phase III may look like:
- Abuse support and education programs for any child or sexual abuse are institutionally supported;
- "Safe Church" policy adopted for local group that is the result of a thorough, documented, and facilitated discussion and education process involving survivors and non-survivors, experts and "average Joes";
- Religious educational programs that integrate experiences of members and help members of church construct meaning from their own experiences.
- Ecumenical efforts to become more functional and competent in preventing child abuse;
- Teams wherein "inside groups" and activists work together, even if it is

additive, like oil and vinegar salad dressing temporarily mixed for a temporary purpose

Phase III may sound like:
- Recognizing and analyzing boundary issues in seminary instruction and formation programs, in parishes, and at diocesan level;
- Compassionate listening and accepting and respecting others' experiences that challenge church views, beginning with abuse victims;
- Facilitated communication about abuse that moves towards dialogue, such as the "truth commission" that has been held in South Africa post-apartheid or between children of Holocaust survivors and children of Nazi soldiers, and now between Israelis and Palestinians.

In phase III, Religious leaders are simply responding justly to problems after they arise. If the Church is truly to be converted in this terrible problem of child sexual abuse, that is, if the Church is truly to "catch fire" and to become Church in its truest, spiritual sense, it will have to move beyond a reactive stance and become active witnesses to its spiritual mission. This is phase IV.

ACT 5.33: COLLECTIVE LEARNING PROCESS – PHASE 3

What have you seen or heard from religious leaders and members relative to Phase III?

How did you respond?

What was the outcome of your action?

THINK: COLLECTIVE LEARNING PROCESS—PHASE 4

Phase IV occurs when the churches become "Victims' Advocates". Just as the churches should be the champion of the poor and the marginalized, they should also be the voice of those who have been devastated by Religious Authority Sexual Abuse. This proactive stance can include a number of actions. A proactive stance will mean preaching and teaching healthy sexuality. There is a need for positive educational programs on human sexuality and for establishing appropriate pastoral boundaries. The churches will need to promote the proper use of power and authority, especially within its own ranks. The churches will want to become a leaven in society to raise consciousness about sexual misconduct issues and to become a force for prevention everywhere.

Phase IV may look like:
- Anticipating healing dynamics; push back as more is learned;
- Active participation in various kinds of organizational change and transformative leadership inter-agency work;
- Attorneys from both groups funding educational and organizational transformation research; research and training that helps the participants assess and improve in the here and now;

- Traveling quilt and photography show regarding abuse healing and transformation, like a kind of moving Museum of Tolerance
- World-centric or integrative stance towards individuals, groups and institutions; living simply so that others may simply live
- Inter-dependence, solidarity and critique; integrative work
- Clergy and "faithful" work as if they were air and water, interdependent and participating in a "precipitation cycle".

Phase IV may sound like:
- Language of discovery and learning with research on abuse and healing;
- Requests for collaboration to better manage known abuse concerns and increase capacity to respond to unforeseen abuse;
- Attorneys from both groups teaching together in law schools and participating in societal questioning and transformation processes to end abuse;
- Multi-directional and inter-institutional reviews of how to end child abuse
- "Remember when children used to be abused? I don't."

ACT 5.34: YOUR CHURCH

Underline any of the following behaviors that relate to your religious community.

- Church officials giving interviews, or speaking to church groups.
- Looking respected in the uniforms of their office.
- Policies or procedures assume that the accused priest must be protected. If he says with great anger that he's misunderstood or innocent of the charges then he is believed and investigations do not go further.
- If no one complains openly to a pastor, nothing is reported to parents, higher-ups or to law enforcement to investigate.

- Shock or sadness that others would accuse or think badly of the Church.
- Righteous anger; defensiveness that the Church is fighting against the powers of evil that seek to destroy it.
- Anger at the media and those who speak publicly about the scandal. Parishioners feeling personally attacked by enemies.

Underline any of the following types of statements that relate to your religious community.

- "We believed the psychologists who said he could return to ministry."
- "The children must have asked for it."
- "They must have been contacted by greedy attorneys who stand to make a lot of money out of their misfortune."
- "They should have said something at the time. Why are they coming forward now?"
- "We were unaware that sexual abuse by clergy happened."

Underline any of the following behaviors that relate to your religious community.
If not these, what other statements relate to your religious environment?

- Pointing the finger at other organizations, like public schools, or society in general.

- Church official is purposely vague when making statements to the press, so as to keep from telling specific lies. See e-mails exchanged between Cardinal Mahony and Vicar for clergy in early days of crisis in L.A.

- Parish or diocesan representative ignores inquiries altogether or doesn't return calls, "forgets" to answer letters or phone calls, or makes excuses for delays.

What is the next step for you in order to be an ally?

SECTION FOUR
WHAT CAN YOU DO?

Finally, what can you do, as a person who wishes to support those who have been abused and as a person who wishes to be aware and skilled enough to protect others from further abuse? First of all, **listen**. Often, when someone shares concern, others try to find a solution to fix the problem. In my example, the problem was framed as "individuals were wounded." The solution became, "fix them." I believe my and others' rage and pain has been a symptom of the problem, not the problem. Victims or survivors need to be heard and the deeper problems related to their experiences must be understood.

Secondly, **learn for yourself.** On our Web site, www.HealingTheSexuallyAbusedHeart.com, there are films, Web sites, articles, books, and conferences for anyone who wishes to act as an effective ally. Before you consider those resources, however, reflect on your own behavior.

I have been part of a professional organization of teacher educators for over ten years. At a recent conference of over 150 teacher education leaders statewide, we were called out by a dean who was heavily involved in the political discussions in his state. He challenged us with the charge that the public and politicians generally do not trust or believe teacher educators with respect to our understanding of teacher preparation, assessment or effectiveness. The anger and hurt in the room was palpable, even after the question and answer period had addressed his harsh statement.

My response to the group in a session I led later relates to our discussion in this chapter. To you, survivor supporters, I ask, "How can survivors of Religious Authority child sexual abuse know of your support, unless you find a more effective way to communicate it?" To my teacher education colleagues, I offered the following.

I think that our speaker was right in his observation. Politicians and many other people do not trust us. My experience is that a person or a group can be trusted when boundaries are clear—when we make it clear who we are, what we want, and what our roles are in relation to others. My sense is that others will believe in us and value what we do when we are consistent.

Parishioners may be shocked that survivors hear SILENCE coming from the people in the pews. How can they know of your support, unless you find a way to communicate it? How do you make it clear who you are, individually and as a group, what you want, and what your roles are in relation to other parishioners, religious leaders, and abuser? My sense is that survivors will believe in you and value what you do when you are consistently present to them, supportive and not abusive towards them, and unashamed of yourself or not shaming of them.

Finally, **make a commitment** to what you have learned. Paulo Freire, one of the most significant social justice educational advocates in our lifetime, spoke of reading the word and the world. The basic step in literacy comes when a person begins to make meaning out of the letters and words. Suddenly, that person does not look at these symbols as meaningless anymore. We do not unlearn our ability to read. Likewise, when a person experiences metanoia, a change of heart, it is as though we are now able to respond in solidarity, albeit a critical solidarity, with the victim and victimizer. We cannot retreat, with integrity, to our simple and perhaps more comfortable state of denial or either-or thinking.

Write what you know about and are willing to do related to the following items:

	What I know	What I am willing to do
"Safe touch or safe church programs."		
Reporting suspected abuse, no matter how vague it might seem or how long ago it might have happened.		
Supporting legislative reform efforts that make it easier for victims to report crimes and pursue their abusers in court.		
Writing and submitting letters to the editor on this subject.		
Finding or creating chances for survivors to speak safely and publicly		
Asking your pastor or others to print material about sexual abuse in church bulletins or publications.		
Thinking of former students, parishioners, and staff who may have lived near or worked around suspected abusers and then discussing the abuse with them.		
Donating to organizations like the National Association to Prevent Sexual Abuse of Children, Bishop Accountability, or Survivors' Network of those Abused by Priests and asking your friends to do the same.		

SUPPORTERS' HEALING WORK

To reclaim our citizenship is to be accountable, and this comes from the inversion of what is cause and what is effect. When we are open to thinking along the lines that citizens create leaders, that children create parents, and that the audience creates the performance, we create the conditions for widespread accountability and the commitment that emerges from it. Accountability is the willingness to care for the well-being of the whole; commitment is the willingness to make a promise with no expectation of return.

In recent history, we have seen disaster photos and headlines displayed across newspaper front pages and crowding minute by minute television and Internet coverage of structural damages ranging from Hurricane Katrina in 2005 to the Minnesota Highway I-35 bridge collapse in 2007. These disasters, while they differ greatly in the scope of loss of life, response time, and other measures, share the fact that the structural threats and problems that gave way were recognized, known, categorized, and pointed out by those with expertise long before people fell into the metaphoric hole in the sidewalk.

Many lives have been destroyed, many people suffered from the immediate disaster and then suffered in invisibility after the immediate attention moved on to another disaster of the day. The problems, the need and understanding were known by leaders and those entrusted with public safety long before the public and political will would be realized to fix the structures or systems that failed. Many of these disastrous environments have still not been substantially changed in order to protect children and vulnerable adults. Many of these environments themselves continue to pose spiritual, emotional, or intellectual health hazards to children and vulnerable adults.

I shared the following with attorneys to share with bishops and diocesan attorneys as they entered into Los Angeles pre-trial discussions in 2007. Many survivors affirmed that it spoke to what they would say to bishops or others who believed that all survivors wanted was a monetary settlement.

"In the known cases alone, we know that many church leaders and religious authorities have sexually abused children or have allowed children to be sexually abused. The lessons from the Vatican and many U.S. bishops show that you are unwilling or incapable of the kind of response that survivors and all affected by child sexual abuse deserve. Your behavior in response to known clergy sexual abuse is exactly the behavior of addicts who abuse themselves and others who care about them, and exactly the behavior of violent abusive parents or partners: denial, remorselessness, a lack of real compassion for victims, a lack of understanding of how much damage you have inflicted (knowingly or unknowingly).

Therefore, the outcome of these "settlements" must not only be a form of "making amends" to the survivors of clergy sexual abuse, but in the form of making amends to society. I propose that you, who have done so much to harm so many, commit to ending child abuse—all child abuse. Everywhere. This is your calling, your path to redemption.

There is no question that you and many members of this community of faith are good people who do and who have done many good things. You are no better than others who have come before you in this regard. Thomas Jefferson, a brilliant "Founding Father", helped construct the constitution that has guided our country over the centuries, and he was a slave owner and he fathered children of his own slaves. He, like you, lived a lie to those he served and perpetuated a social cancer and double standard that continues today in this country on this day that we celebrate our "independence". He was no authority on ending slavery in this country and you are no authority on ending clergy sexual abuse in your church.

End all child abuse —everywhere— and begin within your "community of faith". You cannot do this alone. You did not begin child abuse. You must, however, live to end it. The words you speak to survivors and all you have damaged and destroyed are completely inadequate. Your actions to end all child abuse, beginning with ending it in your ranks, are inadequate. But they are what will matter after today. They will answer the questions that you must answer with your lives, "So what?" So what, that you have fought to release known criminals? So what that you have spent millions of dollars in legal fees to block the truth about child sexual abuse in your lives? So what if you have sold some properties to "settle these cases"? So what if you have avoided bringing the cesspool of child rape in which you walk to a public court?

Your actions to end all child abuse, beginning with ending it in your ranks, will be inadequate. But they are what will answer the question, "Now what?" Now what is different? Now what do we have to show that religious authorities are part of the solution and not the problem of child abuse? Now what will happen the next time a child or adult comes forward to report the unspeakable crime that I and these survivors have reported? These are the questions that you must answer with your actions beginning today: So what? Now what?

Whatever you say and whatever you do, I and other survivors and members of other churches and other countries will ask. So what? Now what?"

This proposition may seem unrealistic. It may not be in our lifetime or in our children's lifetime or in our children's children's lifetime that child sexual abuse everywhere is ended. We will only know the impact of our lives towards this end when we have evidence of efforts to end child sexual abuse anywhere. Words and intentions are completely inadequate at this point to share with those who have been victimized as children or vulnerable adults and then re-victimized by those to whom they reached out for support, validation, or acceptance.

ACT 5.41: DIALOGUE AND COMMIT

Meet with at least one other person whom you consider an ally for RASA survivors and discuss the following questions.

- How can you, as a survivor supporter, take care of yourself? What can you do apart from directly working with victims or survivors to help promote or share the burden of this learning (DK DK)? To help others wake up?

- "Ignorance is bliss" relates to the truth that deep learning brings with it a burden of responsibility. The bad news is the burden of learning; the good news is a deeper level of spiritual understanding and freedom to deal with ambiguity. What's the good news and bad news about your learning and development?

- What do you need to continue in this learning? How can you get some of these needs met with other survivor supporters? What's next? Compare your reflections at the beginning of the chapter regarding how you see yourself as an advocate?

REFLECT: BECOME THE CHANGE

This chapter has identified the key aspects of how the dynamics that sustain or promote Religious Authority Sexual Abuse operate in groups and institutions, such as churches. The chapter has focused on you and your role as a supporter of someone who is recovering from sexual abuse. As a supporter of someone who is recovering from sexual abuse, your awareness of or sensitivity to the problem of religious authority sexual abuse is necessary, although not sufficient, to be an effective ally or change agent.

As a result of reading, thinking and working with this material, I hope that you are now more able to learn for yourself, and to stand more and more on your own as an adult. I hope that you will be more able to bring your own direct experiences with church leaders, parishioners and victims into perspective in a way that leads you to be more of the solution and less of the problem of Religious Authority CSA. As a contemplative in action, and not contemplative inaction, I hope you are more able to observe your own thinking and behavior. Observing is different from judging motives.

I hope you will continue to ask yourself the questions you have been working with: How does this description relate to my organization? What role do I take up in this kind of organization: cheerleader, oblivious bystander, guilty bystander, ally?

Underneath these questions, I believe it is important for you to clarify: What do I want for myself and others in this organization? What can I do to get more of what I want for myself and others in this organization? What might be the consequence(s) of not taking action?

I think it is important to recognize that we are all on a learning curve. Recognizing the ways that you are still learning and growing is important. Such recognition does not negate your goodness, your intelligence, or you intention to help. There is no point in beating up on yourself and others for not being fully free, or fully integrated as humans.

In fact, if we use this information to judge and condemn, we will accomplish the opposite of what we intend, which is to encourage people, especially Catholics, that they can grow up in their faith and stand on their own as mature adults in their relationship to God and the church, just as they do in other areas of their lives where they view themselves as competent adults. The reality is that such emotional, intellectual and spiritual maturity is what will transform what may be the most unspeakable and toxic chapters in church history. With this in mind, commit to doing something each week and then to following up with others on the impact of your action. Become the change in the world that you wish to see.

CHAPTER SIX
DEFINITIONS

DEFINITIONS

CHAPTER ONE

Authority: An explicit or implicit agreement by which power is conferred in return for a service.

Boundaries: Appropriate limits that help us maintain our integrity and integrated, connected sense of self.

Flexible/flexibility: The ability to change your mind and adjust to a new idea.

Happy: Enjoying a particular time or life experience. On the other hand, contentment is a more static state of being at peace with life experiences.

Heal: Become more complete, fully alive.

Incomprehensible: Beyond our understanding.

Indefensible: Unable to resist against or justify.

No talk: Implicit or explicit agreement to stay silent about something important.

RASA: Religious Authority Sexual Abuse

Recovery: Getting and staying healthy.

Role: A formal or informal position in a relationship or organization that serves a purpose, conscious or unconscious, in that relationship or organization.

Shame: The feeling that there is something unacceptable in or about us.

Sponsor: Someone who knows more than you do about recovery and who will hold you accountable to being honest and getting healthy.

Transformation: The practice of changing habits and ways of understanding new ideas.

Voice: The ways we stand up for ourselves or others.

CHAPTER TWO

Acting purely: Acting with a commitment to your best self.

Agency: Ability to act or create.

Child: Someone who is physically, emotionally, intellectually and spiritually underdeveloped and vulnerable.

Control: Management, containment, whether it be physically, socially, or emotionally enforced.

Denial: Refusal to accept.

Hope: Connection to spirit.

Incompleteness: Missing important ingredients or details.

No talk: Implicit or explicit agreement to stay silent about something important.

Perfection: The illusion of being without flaw or error; perfection actually means whole.

Purpose: Goal.

Re-victimization: When a survivor's past trauma is triggered by a current experience.

Roles: Patterns of behaviors; functions that individuals take up, consciously or unconsciously, with others.

Saboteur: A person who acts out by disrupting or derailing what is going on around him or her, or in his or her own life.

Self-victimization: When a survivor's own actions or thinking lead to her own suffering.

Self-worth: The value we put on our own spirit.

Unreliability: Unable to be trusted because behavior is inconsistent or contradictory.

Victim: Someone who is unsuspectingly hurt by another.

CHAPTER THREE

Assess: Make observations about something without applying a value, such as good or bad.

Integrate: Bringing together what was previously fragmented in a way that creates wholeness.

Intentionality: What guides our best self, whether conscious or unconscious.

Object-subject relationship: Seeing ourselves and other people or objects as separate sources.

PTSD: Post Traumatic Stress Disorder
Subject-subject relationship: Seeing ourselves and others as equal sources of agency.
Survivor-victims: Those who are moving beyond "victimhood" and are intentionally reconstructing their identities.

CHAPTER 4

Articulate/articulation: Communication, expression.
Coherence: Clear connection between the various parts.
Generativity: Life-producing, whether symbolic or material.
Palpable: Able to be felt.

CHAPTER 5

Change agent: A person who works to bring a change in the quality of life of another person, group or organization.
Ego-centric: Based upon one person's experience.
Liturgy: Worship service.
Pedophiles: People who sexually abuse children.
SNAP: Survivors' Network of Those Abused by Priests.
Systemic: Relating to the integrated and whole system.

REFERENCES

Ainscough, Carolyn & Toon, Kay. *Surviving childhood Sexual Abuse: Practical self-help for adults who were sexually abused as children.* Cambridge: Da Capo Press, 2000.

Arntz, William, Chasse, Besty, & Vicente, Mark. *What the Bleep Do We Know!?* Deerfield Beach, Health Communications, Inc., 2005.

Bass, Ellen & Davis, Laura. *The courage to Heal: A Guide for Women Survivors of Child Sexual Abuse.* New York: HarperCollins Publishers Inc., 1992.

Block, Peter. *Community: The Structure of Belonging.* San Francisco: Barrett-Koehler Publishers, Inc., 2008.

Chopra, Deepak, M.D. *Overcoming Addictions: The spiritual Solution.* New York: Three Rivers Press, 1997.

Chopra, Deepak, M.D. & Simon, David, M.D.. *The Seven Spiritual Laws of Yoga.* Hoboken: John Wiley & Sons, 2004.

Doyle, Thomas P., Sipe, A.W.R., & Wall, Patrick J. *Sex, Priests, and Secret Codes: The Catholic Church's 2,000 Year Paper Trail of Sexual Abuse.* Los Angeles: Volt Press, 2006.

Freire, Paulo. *Pedagogy of the Oppressed.* New York: Continuum Press, 1985.

*Galasso, Carmine. *Crosses: Portraits of Clergy Abuse.* New York: Trolley Books, 2007.

Gladwell, Malcolm. *Blink: The Power of Thinking without Thinking.* New York: Little, Brown, and Company, 2005.

Hanh, Thich Nhat. *Being Peace.* Berkeley: Parallax Press, 1987.

Howard, Gary. *We Can't Teach What We Don't Know.* New York: Teachers' College Press, 1999.

King, Martin Luther, Jr. *Letters from A Birmingham Jail.* Stamford: Overbrook Press, 1968.

Kivel, Paul. *Men's Work: How to Stop the Violence That Tears Our Lives Apart.* Center City: Hazelden, 1992.

Lama, Dalai and Mansfield, Vic. *Tibetan Buddhism and Modern Physics: Toward a Union of Love and Knowledge.* West Conshohocken: Templeton Press, 2008.

Lawrence, Brother. *The Practice of the Presence of God, and The Spiritual Maxims.* New York: Cosimo Classics, 2006.

McConnell, Patty. *A Workbook for Healing: Adult Children of Alcoholics.* San Francisco: Harper and Row, 1986.

Myss, Caroline. *Sacred Contracts: Awakening Your Diving Potential.* New York: Three Rivers Press, 2003.

Nelson, Portia. *There's a Hole in My Sidewalk.* Hillsboro: Beyond Words Publishing, 1993.

Podles, Leon, J. *Sacrilege: Sexual Abuse in the Catholic Church.* Baltimore: Crossland Press, 2008.

Poling, James N. *The Abuse of Power: A Theological Problem.* Nashville: Abingdon Press, 1991.

Romo, J., Bradfield, P., & Serrano, R. Co-editors. *Reclaiming Democracy: Multicultural Educators' Journeys toward Transformative Teaching.* Columbus: Prentice-Hall, 2004.

Ruiz, Don Miguel. *The Four Agreements: A Practical Guide to Personal Freedom, A Toltec Wisdom Book.* San Rafael: Amber-Allen Publishing, 2001.

Siegel, Bernie S. *Peace, Love and Healing: Bodymind Communication & The Path to Self-Healing.* New York: Harper and Row, 1989.

Tolle, Eckhart. *A New Earth: Awakening to Your Life's Purpose.* New York: Plume, 2005.

Williamson, Marianne. *A Return to Love: Reflections on the Principles of a Course in Miracles.* New York: HarperCollins Publishers, 1992.

Woititz, Janet G. Ed.G. *Adult Children of Alcoholics.* Deerfield Beach: Health Communications, 1990.

Woodson, Carter G. *The Mis-education of the Negro.* New York: Classic House Books (first printed in 1933), 2008.

DEFINITIONS

Dr. Jaime J. Romo

The author grew up in Northeast Los Angeles, and although he lived in a rough neighborhood and contended with different kinds of violence and abuse, he attended Loyola High School and went on to Stanford University, where he earned a bachelor's degree in history in 1981.

He spent three years preparing for ordination at St. John's Theologate before he began teaching Social Studies and Ethics at St. Bernard's High School in Playa Del Rey. He then moved into the Los Angeles Unified School District as an ESL / Bilingual Social Studies teacher, completed a teaching credential at Mount St. Mary's College and then a Master's degree in education with an administrative services credential from the University of California at Los Angeles in 1988.

He completed his doctorate in Educational Leadership at the University of San Diego in 1998, while teaching at National University in the Teacher Education Department. Subsequently, he built upon his multilingual, multicultural and spiritual background in the Department of Learning and Teaching at the University of San Diego, where he prepared outstanding teachers for service in the complex international, global, San Diego-Tijuana region. Dr. Romo brings 24 years of K-12 and university education experience to these pages.

Since 2002, he has taken an active role in education, reconciliation and healing efforts in southern California independently, as well as through the Survivors' Network of those Abused by Priests, (SNAP), the United Church of Christ, and the Faith Trust Institute. He has been the subject of a numerous radio, newspaper, and magazine interviews. He is one of the subjects in the book "Crosses: Portraits of Clergy Abuse," by Carmine Galasso.

Share your thoughts on this book & possibly win prizes.
Everyone who shares ideas on how to make this workbook better
will get a free copy of the next edition of the book.
Go to www.HTSAH.com or www.HealingTheSexuallyAbusedHeart.com